THE WORLD OF
CHARLES RICKETTS

THE WORLD OF
CHARLES RICKETTS

by

JOSEPH
DARRACOTT

METHUEN
New York Toronto

Library of Congress Cataloging in Publication Data
Darracott, Joseph
    The World of Charles Ricketts.
    1. Ricketts, Charles S., 1866–1931. 2. Artists—
England—Biography. I. Title.
N6797.R5D37 1980   709'.2'4   [B]   80–13989
ISBN 0–416–00711–2

First American Edition

Published in the United States by
Methuen, Inc.
733 Third Avenue,
New York, N.Y. 10017

Produced by Cameron & Tayleur (Books) Limited
25 Lloyd Baker Street, London WC1X 9AT.
Text set by Input Typesetting, London.
Colour reproduced by Gateway Platemakers, London.
Monochrome reproduction, printing and binding by
R. J. Acford, Chichester.

Designed by Tom Carter   House Editor: Elisabeth Cameron

Printed and bound in Great Britain

PICTURE SOURCES

Aberdeen Art Gallery: 65a
The Ashmolean Museum, Oxford: 65c, 73
Atkinson Art Gallery, Southport: 107
Author's Collection: 33, 34a, 35, 36a
BBC Hulton Picture Library: 19, 58, 59, 115a & b, 154,
    162, 163a, b, c, 164
By courtesy of Birmingham Museums & Art Gallery: 21
British Library: 191
The British Museum: 74a, 84, 139, 141, 142, 144, 145,
    147, 148a & b, 149, 167, 177, 192
Carlisle Museum & Art Gallery: 65b, 72
Carter Nash Cameron: 18, 28b, 29, 30
Castle Museum, Nottingham: 60, 150b
Courtauld Institute of Art: University of London: 12,
    27, 28a, 36b, 41c, 43, 51, 54b, 62, 100a, 113, 132, 184,
    187
Exeter City Council Museums Service: 138, 175
The Fine Art Society, London: 66
Fitzwilliam Museum, Cambridge: 65c, 74b, 76, 80, 83,
    88, 94b, 100b, 101, 102, 116a & b, 118, 119,
    120a & b, 121a & b, 125, 126a & b, 127, 128, 129,
    130a & b, 131, 133a, b, c, d, 134, 146
Copyright, The Frick Collection, New York: 114

Philippa Lewis: 38
Lincolnshire Museums: Usher Gallery, Lincoln: 166
City of Manchester Art Galleries: 44
Raymond Mander & Joe Mitchenson Theatre
    Collection: 170, 171a, b, c, 172a, 173, 174a & b, 178,
    179, 181, 183, 185a & b, 186, 188, 189, 190a, 194
The Mansell Collection: 16, 90, 92, 93, 94a, 106, 136
Reproduced by courtesy of the Trustees, The National
    Gallery, London: 86, 94a, 95, 109, 124
The National Gallery of Canada, Ottawa: 71, 152, 155,
    156, 157, 159, 160, 161
National Portrait Gallery: 13, 17, 22, 23, 104
Private Collection. (Albums): 8, 9a & b, 10, 11, 15, 26,
    45a & b, 55, 57a & b, 78a & b, 79, 82, 85, 110, 111
Private Collection: 61, 63a & b
Richmond upon Thames Libraries: 25
Scottish National Gallery of Modern Art: 190b & c
Isabella Stewart Gardner Museum: 135
Taranman Gallery, London: 54a
The Tate Gallery, London: 67, 69, 70, 75
Victoria & Albert Museum: 34b, 39a, b, c, 40, 41a & b,
    42, 47, 48, 49, 52, 53, 150a & b
Walker Art Gallery, Liverpool: 172b
Reproduced by permission of The Trustees of the
    Wallace Collection: 97, 98, 105
Warwick District Council Art Gallery & Museum: 122

Contents

Acknowledgements

I have received much help and encouragement from both sides of the Atlantic since I first began to take an interest in the taste and achievements of Charles Ricketts and Charles Shannon. I place first the kindness of Miss Henrietta Sturge Moore and Mr Daniel Sturge Moore, with whose permission copyright material is reproduced. I have also to thank the Trustees of the National Gallery of Canada, who have allowed publication of copyright material from their archive, and members of the Gallery's staff, in particular Dr R. H. Hubbard. Two Directors of the Fitzwilliam Museum, Mr David Piper and Professor Michael Jaffé have enabled me to study the Ricketts and Shannon collection there, and members of the Fitzwilliam staff have been most helpful, as will be evident both in this book and more especially in the catalogue for the 1979 exhibition *All for Art*, where their scholarship elucidates the significance of the items.

I should also like to record my thanks to the late Mrs Ursula Bridge, and the late Ifan Kyrle Fletcher, Mr Malcolm Cormack, Miss Jeanine Bouriau, Mr Duncan Robinson, Mr David Scase, Professor Francis Haskell, Professor Alan Bowness, Professor William Gullens, Professor Marcia Allentuck, Mr Lawrence Smith, Mr Henri Locard, Mr Cecil Lewis, Mr Simon Reynolds, Mr Stephen Calloway, the late Miss Helen Binyon, Mrs Shirley Bury, and the late Mrs Lavinia Handley-Read. I am especially grateful to Mr Paul Delaney, whose biography of Charles Ricketts we look forward to seeing.

The idea for this book was that of Miss Bettina Tayleur. My thanks to her and also to Miss Philippa Lewis who has done the picture research. I hope those people I have mentioned here and others who have helped to bring this project to fruition will feel repaid by some enjoyment of the result.

An Aesthetic Partnership

Charles Ricketts was the prevailing figure in an aesthetic partnership that was unique in the history of art. For nearly fifty years from their student days in Lambeth, he and Charles Shannon lived in a distinctive way as aesthetes or, rather, as men of arts and letters. Their initial close collaboration on the design of books led to the major enterprise of the Vale Press.

In the 1890s, while Ricketts designed books, Shannon was establishing a reputation as a painter and drawing lithographs that were described by a friend and competitor, William Rothenstein, as the most remarkable things done at the time. Shannon's portraits and figure compositions earned him distinction before the First World War. By that time, Ricketts had designed some admirable jewellery, ventured into sculpture, started oil painting, carried out some stage and costume design, and published three books on art. His predominant activity in the 1920s was work for the stage, notably the sets and costume for the first performance of George Bernard Shaw's *Saint Joan*. Alongside their own artistic development, Ricketts and Shannon built up a collection of treasures which eventually contained Egyptian, Greek and Roman antiquities, carved gems, Japanese prints and drawings, some notable European paintings and an outstanding collection of old master drawings by such artists as Titian, Tintoretto, Rubens, Van Dyck, Rembrandt and Watteau, together with a significant group of nineteenth-century drawings by artists including Delacroix, Millet, Rossetti, Burne-Jones and Puvis de Chavannes. The artists' connoisseurship was acknowledged in another way by the appointment of Ricketts as art advisor to the National Gallery of Canada.

Neither Ricketts nor Shannon was a major artist, but the quality of their work is still underestimated. Some signs of a reassessment occurred in 1979, when there appeared within a short space of time a television film, an exhibition of work by Ricketts and Shannon (following a show of Shannon's lithographs in the previous year), an essay on Ricketts accompanying a book of plates and, at the Fitzwilliam Museum, Cambridge, an exhibition of items from their collection. With the present enthusiasm for Art Nouveau and a steadily increasing interest in Victorian art, their reputations are likely to revive. More than that, their lives and activities throw light on a whole period of art and letters.

Few men of their time were comparably versatile. William Morris's range can be likened to that of Ricketts, although against Morris's political activity has to be set Ricketts's more private pleasures of connoisseurship and collecting, and Morris's fame as a poet outstrips Ricketts's achievement in his enjoyable but little known or unpublished journals, stories and dialogues. Morris took no part in the theatre, where Ricketts was highly esteemed. Thomas Sturge Moore quoted Shaw's opinion of 'the noble Ricketts who always acts *en grand seigneur*', while Yeats wrote that his friend was 'in our tradition the last great representative'. Ricketts also had the respect, if not always the agreement or admiration of famous contemporaries. In the 1890s he exerted, as did Beardsley, a powerful influence on his fellow book illustrators; in his theatre work he counted as a rival to Edward Gordon Craig; as a critic he can be compared with his exact contemporary, Roger Fry; as a connoisseur he could contest the views of Bernard Berenson. Perhaps it is not so surprising that Yeats, with Irish hyperbole, should have described Ricketts as a universal genius.

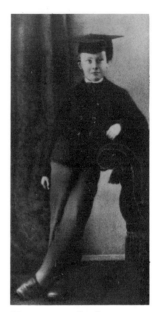

Shannon as a schoolboy.

Yeats's was a minority view. Ricketts and Shannon have for decades remained shadowy and elusive figures, partly because of a strain of personal reticence in both their characters. They are mentioned in many London memoirs of the 1890s and in books about the private press movement, or about art and theatre between 1900 and 1930. The tantalising quality of these glimpses of the two men is made more intriguing by the dazzling variety of references to people and events in *Self-Portrait*, a selection from Ricketts's journals and letters published in 1939. Even the main source of information about Ricketts and Shannon is far from complete – their papers preserved in the British Library only partly document their lives and activities.

Some questions about the artists remain unanswered. One of the unsolved questions, in my view, is the nature of the friendship between the two men. That they loved each other is certain, but from that fact no conclusion can be drawn. There is plentiful evidence of their rapport, which was described by Thomas Sturge Moore as the most perfect relationship he had known. Lord Clark has recently written 'Shannon was quiet and recessive, but his rare interpolations showed good sense and considerable learning. One could see that Ricketts turned to him as to a reasonable wife.' As in a marriage, there were stresses, one of which Ricketts mentions in his diary of 1917, referring to Shannon and an un-named tragic person. Was it mere restlessness that made Ricketts put into an aphorism 'A friend can tire of unremitting sympathy, preferring the unknown of chance meetings' (*Un ami se lasse d'une sympathie trop constante, il préfère à celà l'imprévu des amitiés de rencontre.*)? Was there a real possibility that Shannon might have married? I doubt that Ricketts would have done so in any circumstances, but to explain this judgement we must return to the artists' beginnings.

Charles Hazelwood Shannon, the elder of the two friends, was born in 1863. He was the son of a clergyman in a living at Quarrington in Lincolnshire, and had three sisters. At St John's School, Leatherhead, he was a good football player, and clearly had a knack for getting on with people, no doubt assisted by his tall, handsome presence. From school he went on to study wood-engraving in Lambeth, where he met Ricketts in 1882. They took rooms together in Kennington Road and, on finishing their training, visited Puvis de Chavannes in Paris to ask his advice about studying there. He did not encourage them to continue their studies in Paris, considering that they would be better advised to start work in London, where they could earn a living through their professional skills, and meanwhile use the time left over to develop their art.

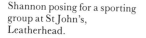

Shannon posing for a sporting group at St John's, Leatherhead.

Ricketts wearing an artist's smock c1888.

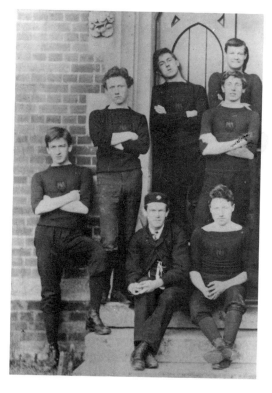

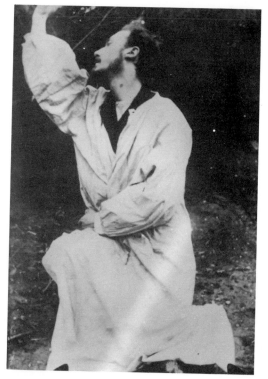

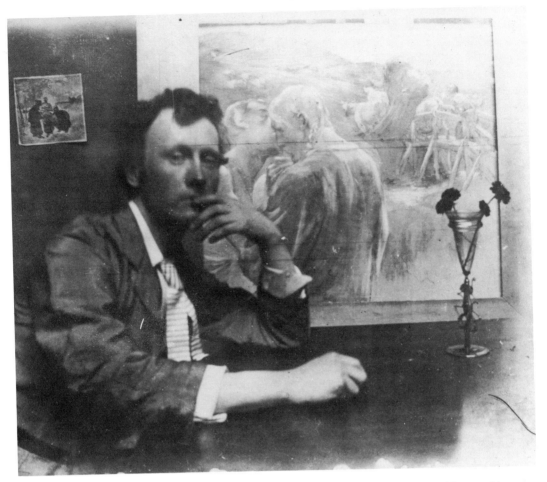

Charles de Sousy Ricketts was born in Geneva on 2nd
October 1866. A small and unathletic boy, the son of a
naval officer, he spent much of his early life abroad with
his mother, Helen de Sousy, a Frenchwoman born in Naples, whose health prevented her from living in England.
Ricketts was with his mother when she died in Genoa in
1880 and returned to London, where his father died two
years later. Ricketts had received little formal education,
although he had attended school in France, but felt inclined
to study art. His grandfather enabled him to do this in
1882, providing a quarterly allowance of £25, and entered
him for training as a wood-engraver at the City & Guilds
Technical Art School in Kennington Road, Lambeth.

It is evident that the two students were markedly different in family background. Shannon always kept in touch
with his family, while mentions of family visits in Ricketts's
diary are often accompanied by the words, 'Cinders. Ashes.
Dust.' Of his sister, who married abroad, there is one
mention in the British Library papers. His sharing of rooms
with Shannon was a natural arrangement between fellow

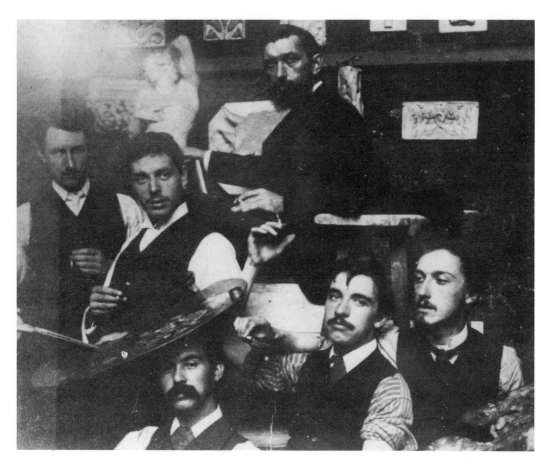

Ricketts with a group of fellow students at Kennington.

students, but for the orphaned Ricketts it was also an emotional anchor.

Three of the artists' friends, Thomas Sturge Moore, Charles Holmes and William Rothenstein, are especially valuable witnesses of their early years. Sturge Moore first met Shannon in Croydon in 1885, when Shannon was teaching at the School of Art. He was the son of a doctor, and his brother was the Cambridge philosopher, G. E. Moore, author of *Principia Ethica*. Thomas Sturge Moore was a poet and writer, whose works on art and aesthetics are directly relevant to our understanding of Ricketts.

He was among the closest friends of Ricketts and Shannon in the 1890s and used to work at the house they rented in The Vale, Chelsea, becoming an editor and illustrator for their Vale Press. Sturge Moore remained a friend after his marriage in 1903 and devoted considerable energy to ensuring that Ricketts was remembered after his death. As Ricketts's literary executor, he preserved the papers from which *Self-Portrait* was edited. His monograph published in 1933 was the only worth-while piece of work available on Ricketts until 1979. In it he describes Ricketts in 1887, the year of their meeting:

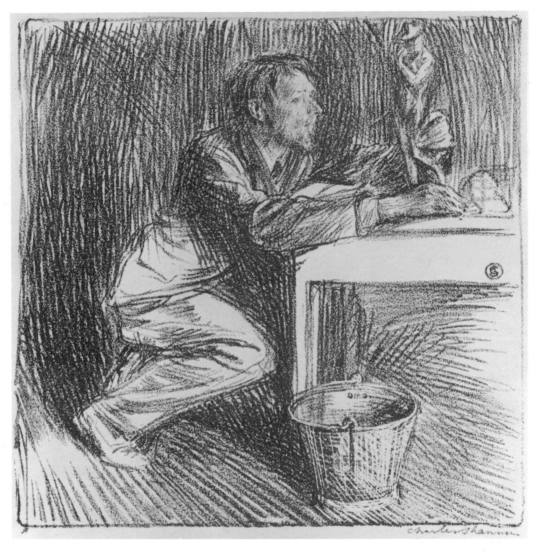

'I saw him, a short, ramshackle youth in a cloud of extremely fine tow-coloured hair which stood around his head
like a dandelion puff. At 11 a.m. he had just turned out of
bed and had no collar, no socks, and just enough on to
enable him to cross the hundred yards from their rooms to
the school. When he entered he was imitating an orchestra
with gestures as well as sounds, a characteristic mode of
progression from room to room, all his life . . .

'I have never met a more energetic or more rapid mind.
Like a motor launch hampered in a crowd of tubs, he was
always producing collisions and soreness; but his extreme
generosity forgot both that you had crossed him and that
he had hurt your pride, before you did. And when he
praised, he praised indeed. He advanced all the time de-
stroying the past . . .

Thomas Sturge Moore as *The
Modeller*, Shannon's first
lithographic portrait, issued in
his set of Early Lithographs in
1893.

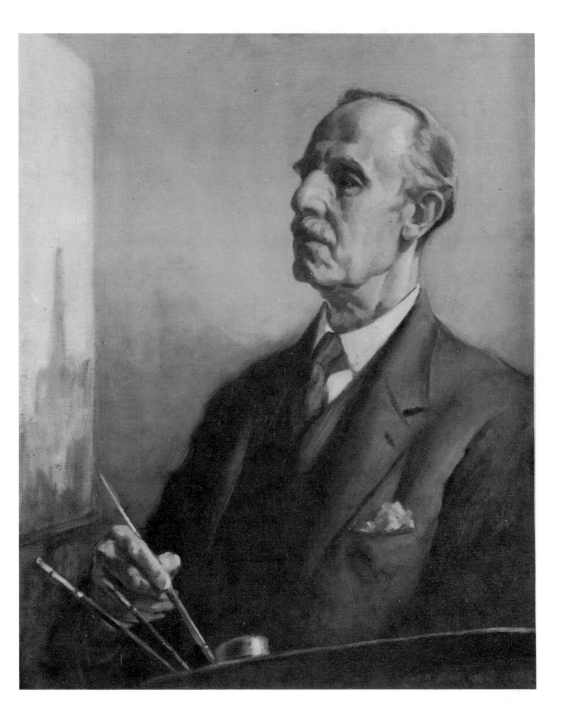

Charles Holmes, a portrait
painted after his retirement as
Director of the National Gallery
by G. H. B. Holland.

'We went to the library at South Kensington every Saturday evening and saw the art journals and expensive publications and soon the old masters began to rise like peaks over the foothills but never became an exclusive object of study. There was no attempt to narrow the field of experience, such as preservation dictates to the majority of tastes.'

This irregular education produced excellent results, and the two artists were able to hold their own in the most demanding company. Sturge Moore was obviously an admirer who owed a great deal to the teaching of his two friends, but his high opinion of the two men was shared by another friend of the 'nineties, Charles Holmes, who found in the company of Ricketts and Shannon a 'flood of witty comment on art and letters' and described the effect of Ricketts on his own career:

'In the matter of reading, my horizon had been widened immensely by introduction to the literature of modern France; in practical aesthetics the influence of Ricketts was more potent still. Before I knew him my judgements had been rough and ready, as well as strongly biased by commonplace handbooks. His refinement of eye and taste, his complete independence, did much to correct my native crudities, compelling much closer attention to small things, a weighing of spiritual and technical qualities in a nicer balance than any I had previously used ... Since their private ambitions involved an intense study of the technique of oil painting, Ricketts and Shannon naturally employed this technical knowledge when criticising pictures and infected me with the same interests. By talking over with them the condition, pigments and handling of works seen in galleries and sale-rooms, I gained in the course of a few years a foundation of practical experience which was afterwards to prove most helpful.'

In his autobiography, Holmes was looking back on a distinguished career. The son of a clergyman, he had won scholarships to Eton and Brasenose College, Oxford, where he had been an admirer of Walter Pater. He started work in London with his cousins' publishing firms of Rivingtons, and worked with the Ballantyne Press and then John C. Nimmo, a specialist in fine editions and remainders. His association with Ricketts and Shannon dated from 1892, and he acted as their business manager when the Vale Press was founded. Holmes always recognised a considerable personal debt to Ricketts, although his own habits of persistent study and careful management of people and affairs were the chief qualities that accounted for a successful career in charge, first, of the National Portrait Gallery and then, in 1915, of the National Gallery. At The Vale in Chelsea and, later, in Beaufort Street, when Ricketts and Shannon were at home to their friends on Friday nights, he was a regular visitor.

The young Holmes did not make a favourable impression on all the guests who visited Ricketts and Shannon. One evening he was unable to think of a suitable comment after Oscar Wilde's reading from the manuscript of *The Sphinx*,

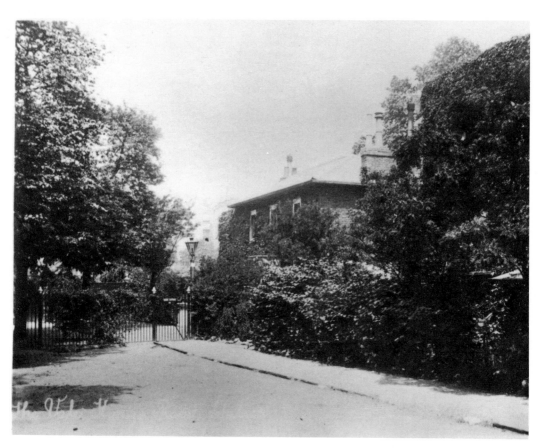

Ricketts and Shannon lived in Whistler's former house, with characteristic decoration such as apple green walls. When they left, the house was taken by Llewellyn Hacon and his wife.

which Ricketts was to illustrate and bind. The windows of the house were open, and Holmes could not help hearing his name mentioned as a new friend when Wilde was leaving. ' "Yes,", said Wilde, "quite nice, but *so* dull."

"No," replied Ricketts bravely. "He is really quite intelligent, but most horribly overworked." '

Holmes provides a vivid picture of a subsequent evening.

'The last appearance of Wilde at The Vale which I remember was also the most brilliant. Walter Sickert was there, boyish, clean-shaven, aureoled with a mass of blond hair, playing with a crinolined doll and flashing out now and then with some witty repartee; Steer sat by me in monumental silence; while Ricketts, perched on the edge of a table engaged Wilde in a long verbal combat. So swiftly came parry and *riposte*, that my slow brain could only follow the thought-play several sentences behind, and I cannot remember a word of what passed, except "Oh! Nonsense, Oscar!" from Ricketts, though it lives in my memory as the most dazzling dialogue which I was ever privileged to hear.'

William Rothenstein, who was to become Principal of the Royal College of Art, is well known to students of

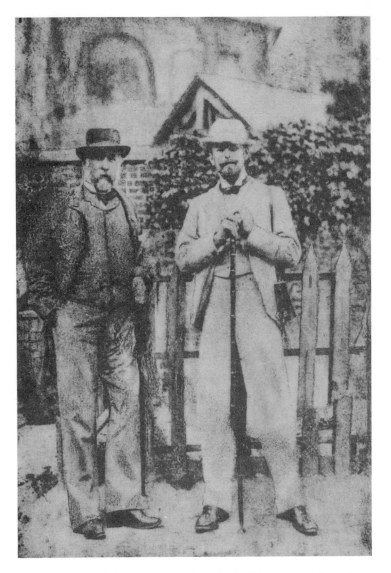

Degas and Sickert by William Rothenstein. Sickert was one of the few Englishmen who knew Degas well, bringing him to life in conversation with his London friends. After Degas' death, Ricketts reflected on 'one of the familiar friends of our boyhood' that 'in a sense, even more than in the case of Whistler, his has been a case of success by *intimidation*, his was the name with which to bludgeon the others.'

British art and letters as an indefatigable memoirist of art and artists in the early part of the twentieth century. It was he who executed the lithograph through which Ricketts and Shannon are readily recalled. This is an attractive and skilful composition, but deceptive in one detail, for it makes the two men appear to be of much the same height, whereas in reality Shannon was tall and Ricketts a diminutive man of little more than five feet.

According to Rothenstein, 'Shannon was as quiet and inarticulate as Ricketts was restless and eloquent. He had a ruddy boyish face, like a countryman's, with blue eyes and fair lashes; he reminded me of the shepherd in Rossetti's *Found*. Oscar Wilde said that Ricketts was like an orchid, and Shannon like a marigold. Ricketts, in giving his opinions, always said "we". The partnership seemed

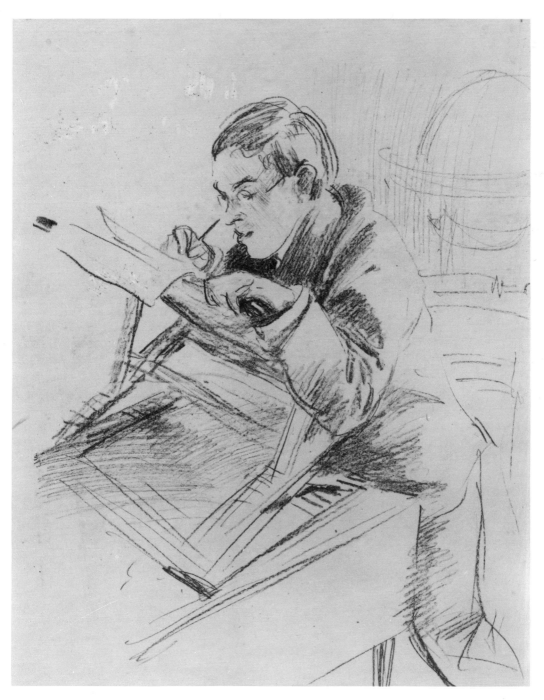

William Rothenstein, 1897, a drawing by J. S. Sargent. The portraitist portrayed – Rothenstein was an untiring portrait draughtsman all his life, his work ranging from Oxford Portraits of the 1890s to portraits of Royal Air Force personalities in the 1940s.

perfect; there was never a sign of difference or discord; each set off the other, in looks as in mind . . . I revered these two men, for their simple and austere ways, their fine taste and fine manners. They seemed to stand apart from other artists of their time; and I was proud of their friendship, so rarely given, and of the encouragement they gave to my work.

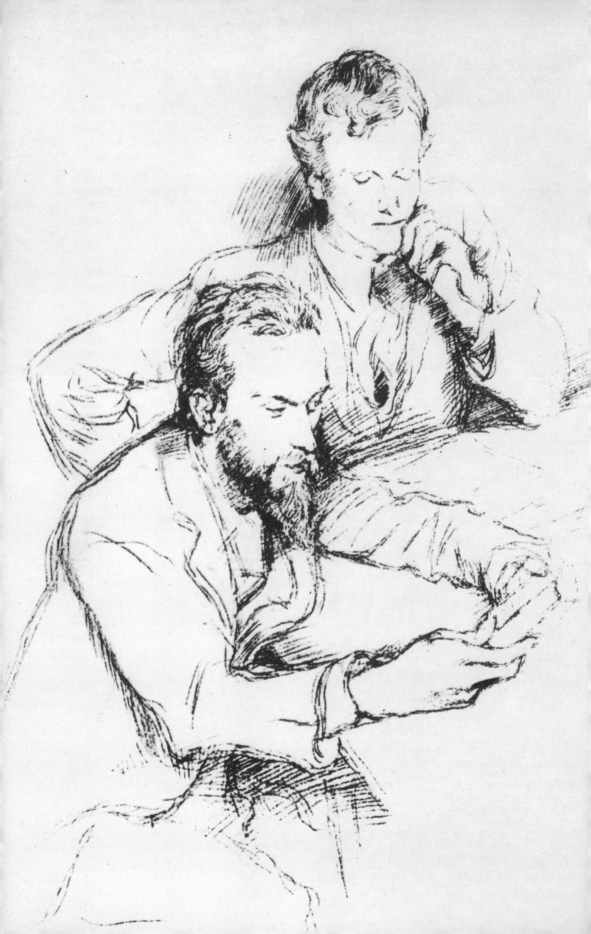

'Shannon was reserved and quietly appreciative, while Ricketts had a passion for influencing others. There is no word to describe this fatal desire, this *Einflusslust.*' Rothenstein even went so far as to liken Ricketts to the Earl of Warwick, king-maker: 'Ricketts's masterful personality dominated all who came into contact with him. The more intellectual draughtsmen, including Beardsley and Laurence Housman, looked to him as their leader. He was in fact the artistic Warwick of the age.'

Ricketts made a cool but not unfriendly assessment of Rothenstein. Describing an evening's conversation in 1904, he commented, 'He talked well on serious subjects; he is the only man besides TSM who will face a serious subject.' Later in the same year, he enlarged on this in a comparison of Rothenstein with Sickert, with whom he had just spent an evening: 'Sickert . . . is the only other intelligent man I have met among British artists (his is the better headpiece). According to their mood the first with his limitations is intelligent, worldly, shrewd and worthy; the other bores one with his wish to make all art in his own image; he remoulds things nearer his own desires.'

Sickert, who also lived in The Vale for a short time.

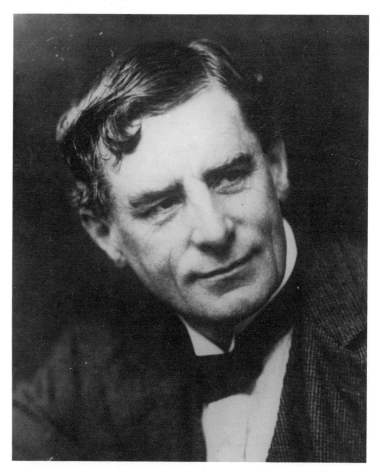

Rothenstein's opinion of the artists was tempered with shrewdness, but he remained greatly attracted to Ricketts and Shannon. 'They were so different from any artists I had met hitherto. Everything about them was refined and austere. Ricketts, with his pale, delicate features, fair hair and pointed gold-red beard, looked like a Clouet drawing. Half French, he had the quick mind and the rapid speech of a southerner. He was a fascinating talker. His knowledge of pictures and galleries astonished me; he had been no-where except to the Louvre, yet he seemed to know every-thing, to have been everywhere. And he knew the names of rare flowers, of shells and of precious stones.'

This enthusiastic account of Ricketts's charm could as easily have been given by two other friends of both the artists and Rothenstein, the poets who wrote in the course of an extraordinary lifelong partnership under the pseu-donym of Michael Field. Katherine Bradley, born in 1846, and her niece, Edith Cooper, who was born in 1862, studied classics together at University College, Bristol, in the 1870s. Katherine Bradley had published a book of her own poetry and had collaborated with Edith Cooper on another by 1884, when the two of them took the decisive step of publishing *Callirrhoe* under the name by which they were afterwards known, Michael Field. *Callirrhoe* received criti-cal approval, especially from Robert Browning, who be-came their staunch supporter. Their devotion to a life of letters was unremitting, in a way which would perhaps have been better understood in France than in England. A sentiment which expresses the basis of their partnership can be found in Rossetti's *Hand and Soul*, a text character-istically published by both the Kelmscott and Vale presses:

'What God hath set in thine heart to do, that do thou; and even though thou do it without thought of Him, it shall be well done. It is this sacrifice that He asketh of thee, and His flame is a sign. Think not of Him, but of His love and thy love.'

Sacrifice became more than a pursuit of letters in the face of critical indifference or hostility. The two poets were fortunate in that financial independence enabled them to continue writing a total of twenty-seven tragedies, eight books of lyrics and a masque. Sacrifice came also to mean conversion to Roman Catholicism.

However, when the two women met Ricketts and Shan-non in 1894, their religious conversion could not have been foreseen. The artists and the poets responded eagerly to each other, developing a tender, somewhat formal relation-ship, in a climate of music and art. Ricketts was a constant critic of their poetry and, for example, commented about

Edith Cooper, pencil drawing by Shannon. A sensitive portrait of the poet which suggests how 'sudden shadows would flit across the face at some inner perception of memory.'

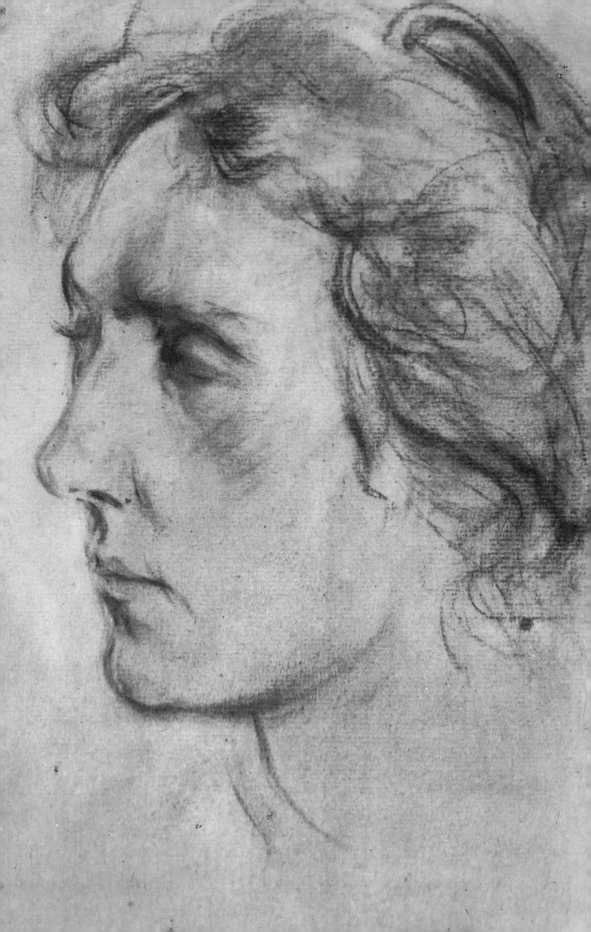

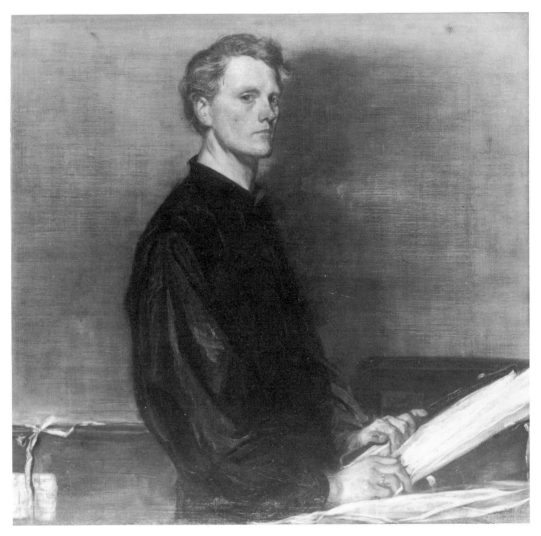

The Man in the Black Shirt, a self portrait by Shannon, 1897.

a poem on Pan, 'The poem has caught not merely much of the actual texture of Keats, but much of the thought or entranced mood.' Many of their exchanges seem precious today, as in Ricketts's letter after receiving from the poets flowers for use in book illustrations, 'I am twining bows of honeysuckle into a border for a Catullus from a portrait by Shannon of a spray you gave me.' Or, after visiting the south coast, 'While staying near Birchington-on-Sea we placed a pot of red lilies on the grave of Dante Gabriel Rossetti and stole from it two wilted tired roses bitten by the sea air.' Ricketts encouraged them to see Shannon's portrait of him (now in the National Portrait Gallery): 'Do not miss seeing my portrait at the New English. I like it much. I am turning away from the 20th century to think only of the 15th.' After the poets had seen it, he wrote again, 'I am glad you like my portrait. I think hereafter it will seem "likely", that is the most one can expect of a

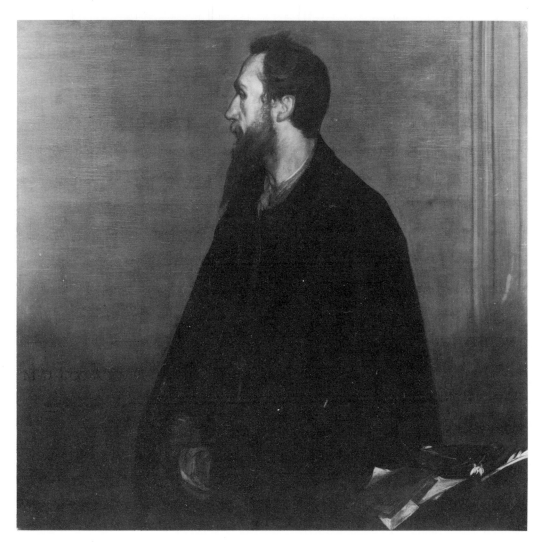

This portrait of Ricketts by Shannon, *The Man in the Inverness Cape*, 1898, was painted as the companion to his self portrait which together form the definitive early portraits of the two artists. The squarish format and understated colour recall Whistler, but the poses are of the Renaissance.

portrait – I look as if I had written to Ariosto, the book at my side has been sent to me by Aretino with a hint that a silk doublet would be acceptable. We are in A.D. 1515.'

The poets were known to their friends as 'Michael' (Katherine Bradley) and 'Henry' (Edith Cooper), and they gave special names to members of their circle. After the simplicity of 'The painters' for Ricketts and Shannon and 'The poets' for Michael Field came more *recherché* names. William Rothenstein's wife was 'Noli', an abbreviation of Christ's injunction *'Noli me tangere'* to Mary Magdalen, while Rothenstein, asked to find a name for himself, thought of the guardian figures of Chinese graves but, not knowing that they were lions, acquired the name of 'The Heavenly Dog'. They sometimes used these names in letters, where Ricketts referred to himself as a lizard or basilisk and, in recounting a conversation with Berenson, remarks that 'the "lamb" skipped into some paradoxes.'

23

Ricketts himself provides a vivid description of 'The poets': 'Michael was small, ruddy, gay, buoyant and quick in word and temper. Henry was tall, pallid, singularly beautiful in a way not appreciated by common people, that is, white with gray eyes, thin in face, shoulders and hands, as if touched throughout with gray long before the graying of her temples.'

For twenty years, the lives of Michael Field and the painters were interwoven. Perhaps the neglect suffered by the poets in their work darkened the hopes of success that Ricketts and Shannon may have entertained, but personally and professionally they maintained a mutual esteem, supporting each other with criticism and encouragement – Ricketts was particularly helpful as a commentator on their dramas. The verse of Michael Field, with its elaborate and formal diction, and a multitude of classical and historical allusions, could even in their own day be understood by only a few of the poets' contemporaries. Theirs was exactly the sort of poetry that was under challenge from the simpler styles of the Georgian poets, or the imagery of the young Ezra Pound. Their most accessible poems are the lyrics, of which this is an example:

> My lady has a lovely rite
> When I am gone
> No prayer she saith
> As one in fear:
> For orison
>
> Pressing her pillow white
> With kisses, just the sacred number,
> She turns to slumber;
> Adding sometimes thereto a tear
> And a quick breath.

Michael Field's poems on themes of paintings, *Sight and Song*, provide an interesting parallel with Ricketts's critical and appreciative writings on art. Their learned plays, in which their wide-ranging scholarship was augmented by Richard Garnett at the Reading Room of the British Museum, show qualities of insight and a sense of pscyhological drama. It was the love of history shared by Ricketts with these writers of *The Tragic Mary* (about Mary Stuart) and *Borgia* that made his gift to the Tate Gallery in their memory – a portrait of Lucrezia Borgia by Rossetti – such a fitting memorial. The comparative success of *Borgia*, published anonymously on Ricketts's advice, leads one to speculate how far the general knowledge of the real identity of 'Michael Field' contributed to the poets' critical neglect.

To infer from the theme of *Long Ago*, inspired by fragments of Sappho and published in 1889, or the warmth of

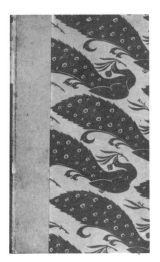

Book binding by Ricketts designed for Michael Field's play, *The World at Auction* (Hacon & Ricketts, 1898). The paper used for this cover is Ricketts' Peacock design.

the love poetry addressed by Michael to Henry, that their relationship was overtly homosexual would be, while understandable, completely to misconstrue the expressive artifice of poetry in the 1890s. The work of Michael Field took inspiration from classical sources, just as Yeats sought to draw on psychic experience. Like Yeats in his early work, Michael Field embellished high-flown sentiment with a special poetic vocabulary. After their reception into the Roman Catholic church, the poets turned from pagan themes to devotional poetry.

For three years both the poets and the painters lived in Richmond. The home of Katherine Bradley and Edith Cooper at the Paragon, as described by Gordon Bottomley, was a suitable setting for their work:

'Their rooms were not less flawless than their poems. Their interiors showed a rarer, wider more certain choice than those of the Dutch painters. The silvery clear lithographs of their friend, Mr C. H. Shannon, were hung all together in a cool northern room, which they seemed to permeate with a faint light; and in another room the golden grain of the walls, alike with the Persian plates that glowed on the table as if they were rich, large petals, seemed to find their reason for being there in the two deeply and subtly coloured pictures by Mr Charles Ricketts on the walls.

'But always there was the same feeling of inevitable choice and unity everywhere; in a jewelled pendant that lay on a satinwood table, in the opal bowl of pot-pourri nearby on which an opal shell lay lightly – a shell chosen for its supreme beauty of form, and taken from a rose-leaf bed by Miss Cooper to be shown to a visitor in the same way as she took a flower from a vase, saying "This is *Iris susiana*" as if she were saying "This is one of the greatest treasures in the world" and held it in her hand as if it were part of her hand.'

The most effective parallel to be found for the lives of Ricketts and Shannon or Michael Field is the literary and collecting partnership of the Goncourt brothers, who were the subject of an article in the first issue of *The Dial*. Ricketts and Shannon were well read. They constantly visited the theatre, opera and ballet, participated in exhibitions and productions, and returned to a home that was full of treasures from every period and many styles. Faced with disappointments they took an ironic stand. Characteristically, Ricketts was prepared to acknowledge Anatole France as a master only after the publication of *Penguin Island* – his sympathy is evident in the aphorism 'True wisdom turns to us a voluptuous and ironic mouth.' (*La vraie sagesse nous montre une bouche voluptueuse et ironique.*)

The Vale Press

For most of the 1890s, Ricketts and Shannon lived in Chelsea, establishing a circle of friends and acquaintances in the worlds of publishing and art. They were known for their magazine, *The Dial*, which first appeared in 1889, and then for their books. After their move to Richmond in 1898, their activities continued in a similar pattern, with Ricketts supervising the production of The Vale Press (until 1903), while Shannon pursued his practice as a painter and, more especially, a portraitist.

Their circumstances in the early part of the 'nineties are well described by Holmes: 'In 1892 they were settling down to an agreed programme which had in it something of the heroic. Shannon, they decided, was to be the great painter.' Two of his early works had been shown in 1887 at the Grosvenor Gallery, but he would not exhibit again 'until he appeared as the complete and undeniable master, upon whose princely income Ricketts then proposed to live in ease for the rest of his life. Until that great day came, Shannon's work would be done in private, watched and criticised by Ricketts alone, and the painter would work

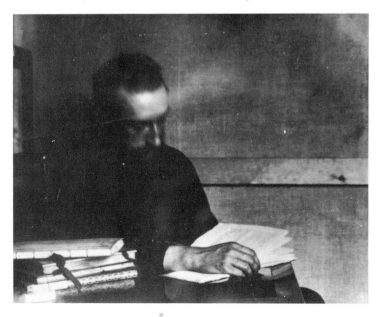

Ricketts with a pile of Vale Press books.

26

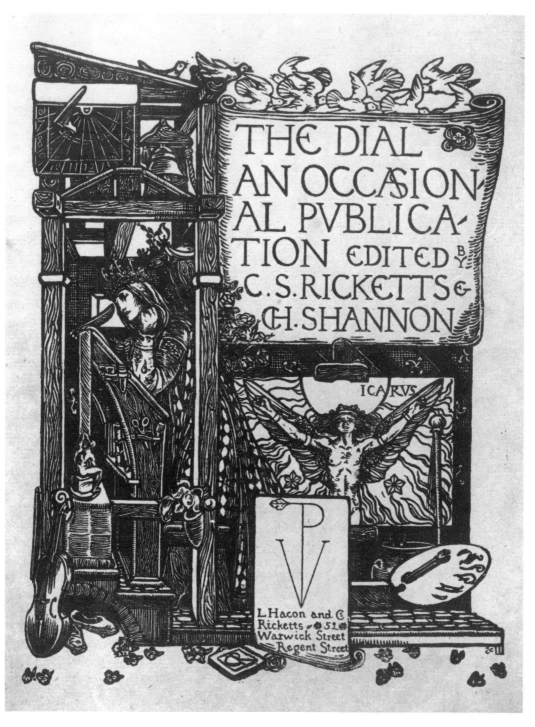

THE DIAL AN OCCASION-
AL PVBLICA-
TION EDITED BY
C.S.RICKETTS &
CH.SHANNON

ICARVS

L.Hacon and C?
Ricketts ☙ 52 ☙
Warwick Street
Regent Street

Ricketts' design for *The Dial* cover, issue no. 5.

for their common welfare only when collaboration was required, or necessity compelled. It was on Ricketts that the main burden was laid of providing for immediate wants, by drawing illustrations, advertisements or anything else which would bring in a little money.'

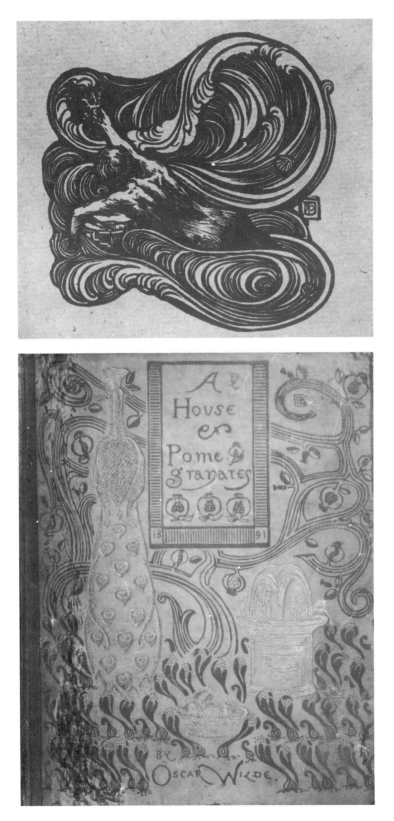

Design for the reverse of *The Dial* cover. (Note, the initials are reversed.)

Ricketts' cover for *A House of Pomegranates* by Oscar Wilde (James R. Osgood McIlvaine, 1891) which the author so firmly defended.

Ricketts's commercial drawing, though competent and versatile, held less significance for the future than the book design which he undertook at this time. A friendship with Oscar Wilde, that had begun when he visited Ricketts and Shannon in The Vale after seeing a copy of *The Dial*, brought the opportunity for Ricketts to design Wilde's own books, followed by other commissions from his publisher, Osgood, McIlvane & Company, and later Elkin Matthews and John Lane. It was in reply to criticism of *A House of Pomegranates* (1891) that Wilde wrote, 'There are only two people in the world whom it is absolutely necessary that the cover should please. One is Mr. Ricketts, who designed it, the other is myself, whose book it binds. We both admire it immensely.' Later in life, writing reminiscences of Wilde in the 1920s, Ricketts felt he had made less than a full estimate: 'It is astonishing that I viewed him as the most genial, kindly and civil of men, but it never entered my head that his personality was the most remarkable I should ever meet, that in intellect and humanity he is the largest type I have come across.'

He also felt that Wilde's eccentricity in appearance had been exaggerated. 'Even today his clothes would pass

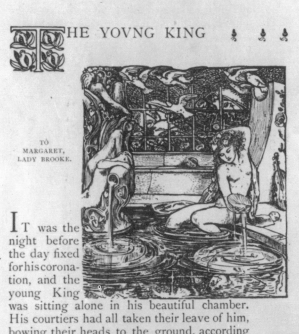

This title page to one of the stories in *A House of Pomegranates* is not remarkable as a *mise-en-page*, but is an attractive early illustration.

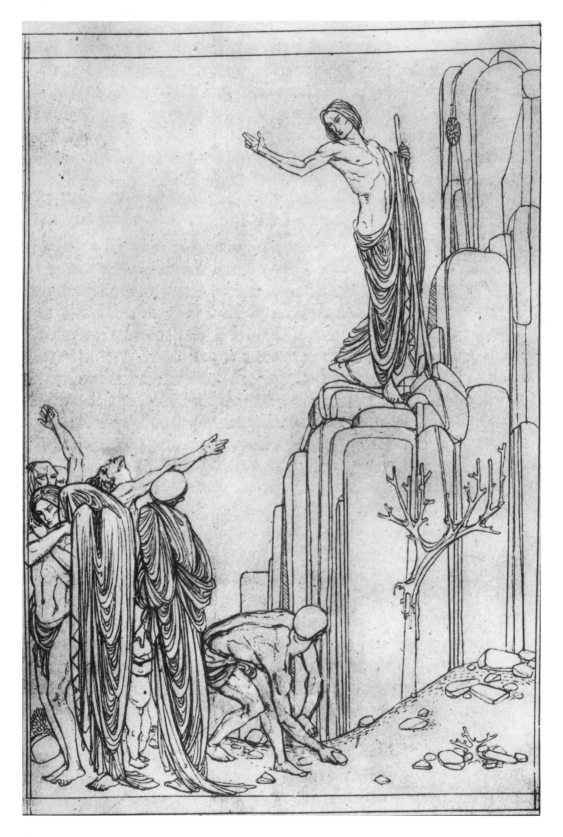

unobserved, a flowing tie seemed foreign, a large button-hole was then the fashion, his old-world stick and scarab ring were alone unusual. There was nothing eccentric as with Whistler, with his yellow tie, wasp-waist, beige coloured overcoat, wand-like stick and flat-brimmed top-hat – such as one sees in early Manets. With Whistler the impression ever remained of a Hungarian band-master aping Mephistopheles.'

The work of Rossetti, an enthusiasm which the two young artists had in common with Wilde, was a strong force in the shaping of their taste. Sturge Moore, writing of events in 1890 or 1891, recalled, 'We lived at the time in the atmosphere, anecdotes and appreciations of Rossetti (of which the sources were Oscar Wilde, probably John Ruskin and Fairfax Murray).' The attraction of Rossetti's work lay in his poetry, his narrative illustrations and his later idealised figures of women. Among the poems, Ricketts thought most highly of *The Portrait* and *The Blessed Damozel*, from which come these short extracts:

'This is her picture as she was:
It seems a thing to wonder on,
As though mine image in the glass
Should tarry when myself am gone.
I gaze until she seems to stir,
Until my eyes almost aver
That now, even now, the sweet lips part
To breathe the words of the sweet heart –
And yet the earth is over her.'

* * *

'The blessed damozel leaned out
From the gold bar of Heaven;
Her eyes were deeper than the depths
Of water stilled at even;
She had these lilies in her hand,
And the stars in her hair were.'

'Her robe, bright from clasp to hem,
No wrought flowers did adorn,
But a white rose of Mary's gift,
For services meekly worn;
Her hair that lay along her back
Was yellow like ripe corn.'

Rossetti's drawings and paintings express in visual terms the idealistic qualities of his poetry. Ricketts was never to lose the admiration he felt for Rossetti in the 'nineties and wrote as late as 1928, 'He is one of the most singular and original men in art: even his latter and most undelectable works, done when he was half-blind and mad with chloral, are unlike anything else.' His persistent admiration was also expressed in purchases of drawings and in the care he took to see that Rossetti was well represented in the national collections (notably on the dispersal of an important collection of his works).

Wilde also shared with Ricketts and Shannon a feeling for the work of Gustave Moreau, in its own way as important an influence as that of Rossetti. Ricketts saw clear differences in attitude between Rossetti and Moreau.

'In an early phase of his art Rossetti has succeeded in painted narrative. He has cast together, under the light of an intense imagination, not only the incidents of some story interwoven with new poetic additions and suggestions, but the almost digressive element of personal predilections in circumstances and counter-incidents; shrinking from no complexity in his certainty of grasp in close-knit design. With Gustave Moreau the dramatic element is also realised, but under different conditions. His creatures would become troubled and shadowy indeed if brought face to face with real facts and passions; they would swoon upon themselves, called back by some faint Lethean murmur or portent. Reality is suggested only by a few fair things fostered in the shadow of palaces, ravines, and by dim rivers, where light, water and air have become resolved into the limpid colours of rare crystals. The evidence of separate life, of the *without*, so hotly insisted on by Rossetti, is reduced by Moreau to the half-fascinated wheeling, the circular flight of a bird, fraught at times with great realistic point, as in the shrieking seamew that flashes across the fall of Sappho from the rocks. His choice is among things of pomp and ritual. In this and his partiality for certain colours will be found his greatest limitations; yet therein is also a sense of voluptuous melancholy which is the whole secret of his fascination.'

Gleeson White, author of a book on illustration in the 1860s and an active figure in the artistic circles of the 'nineties, was co-editor with Shannon of a magazine *The Pageant*, of which two volumes appeared in 1896 and 1897. In the second, he wrote an article which dealt with this theme of idealism and, in passing, refused to accept for Moreau the epithet of 'the French Burne-Jones'. He went on to explain the distinction, 'For Moreau is the classic ideal, which is scholarly simplicity; although in his case it is often overlaid with the fantastic decoration of the earlier mythologies whence Greece drew its inspiration. Burne-Jones is the romantic ideal, with its Christianity and Paganism blended in the twilight of the gods – the transitional time when the early church buried the marble statues of Venus lest at night she should awaken and tempt their

Gustave Moreau: *The Apparition* from *The Pageant*, 1897. 'Salomé seems already conscious of the doom between her and the face whose nimbus grows in the declining daylight, as the dawn might grow on a blind when the lamp goes out; beyond, the sky centres to a blood-like spot, half-cloud, half garment of the executioner passing beyond, like a fearful messenger to God.'

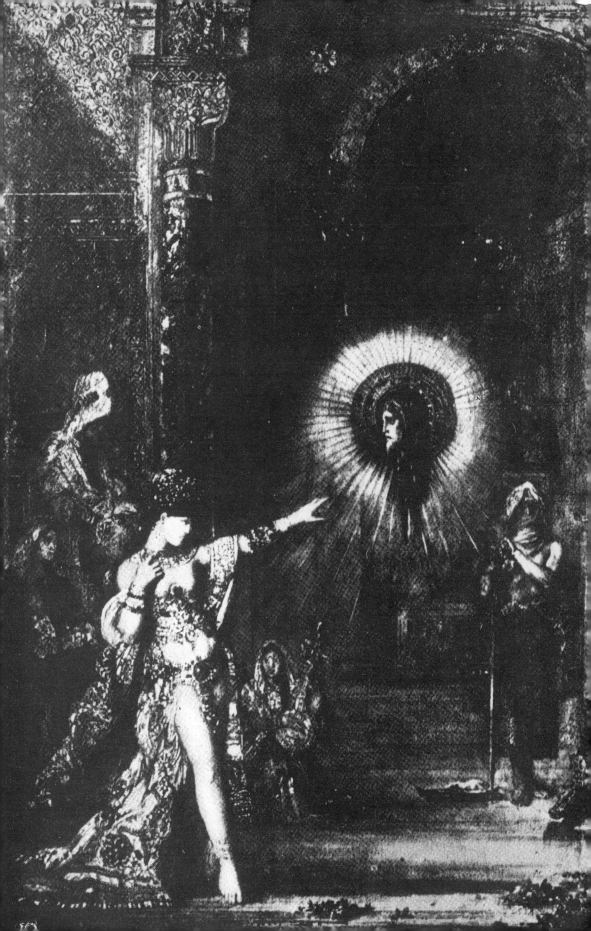

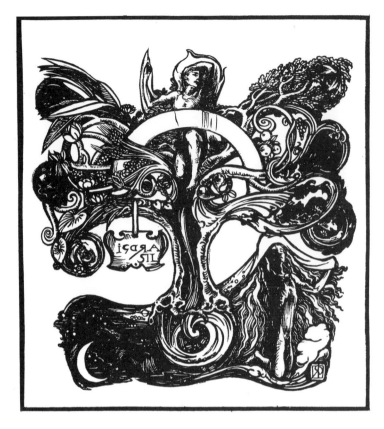

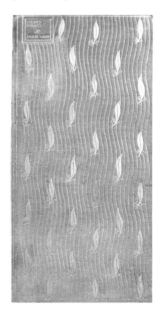

proselytes astray.' The difference between the two artists
is illustrated in the plates, which include *The Apparition*,
Moreau's famous picture of Salome seeing the head of St
John the Baptist in a vision, described by Huysmans in his
book *À Rebours* and shown in England at the first exhibition
of the Grosvenor Gallery. Burne-Jones's work is represented by two paintings on the theme of Perseus.

The work of these artists, Rossetti, Burne-Jones and
Moreau, was central to the eclectic taste expressed by
Ricketts and his friends in *The Dial* and *The Pageant*. *The
Dial* appeared first in 1889 and then in 1892, 1893, 1896
and 1897. The other indispensable element was admiration
for some current French literature, especially works by
Baudelaire, Verlaine, Villiers de I'Isle Adam and Huysmans, all of whom had to be added to Holmes's English
and classical education. John Gray's *Silverpoints*, a book of
poems, including translations from Verlaine, Rimbaud and
Mallarmé, was characteristic of the period. The title refers
to silverpoint, (a drawing medium which Alphonse Legros
used for portraits of Ricketts and Shannon). The book was
exquisitely designed by Ricketts, using a long thin format
referred to as a saddle book, and the cover was gilded with
a repeating flame motif that was widely imitated, as a

pattern in textiles, for example. Gray wrote about *Les Goncourt* in the first number of *The Dial* and contributed an article on Huysmans in the fourth. In the second number, Sturge Moore's poetry was complemented by an article of his on Maurice de Guérin.

Before 1895 their interest in French poetry and English visionary art placed Ricketts and Shannon in the avant garde. That year saw the trial of Oscar Wilde, which left many artists and writers feeling that idealism and sensitivity for new strains of art had become tarnished through association with Wilde's homosexual practice; and subsequently men of art and letters (though not Ricketts and Shannon, who were among the few friends who tried to help Wilde after his spell in prison) pharisaically avoided ideas which he seemed to represent. Ricketts wrote that events had left a bitter taste – 'Something happened from which I have never quite recovered, a mistrust of the British conscience, a mistrust of modern civilisation.' Different ideals, notably realism in literature and Impressionism in art had gained a stronger hold by the beginning of the twentieth century.

Such ideals were not attractive to the Vale artists who admired, for instance, Blake, on whose work Shannon's first handwritten title for *The Dial* was based, or another English artist, Edward Calvert, who inspired illustrations by Sturge Moore. Both magazines amounted to a statement of the artistic and literary preferences shared by a group of friends and also, as we shall see, provided opportunities for critical and historical writing on subjects like Japanese prints, or wood-engraving (about which Ricketts wrote in a personal but highly informed way in *The Pageant*).

Woodcut by Edward Calvert. Interest in Edward Calvert was of a piece with enthusiasm for William Blake, whose illustrated poems made the Vale group think more deeply about book design and illustration.

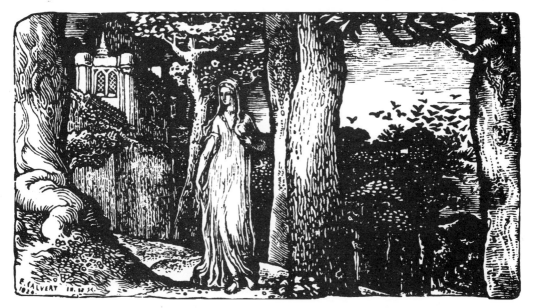

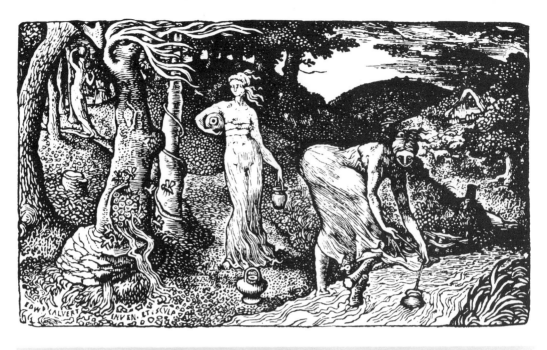

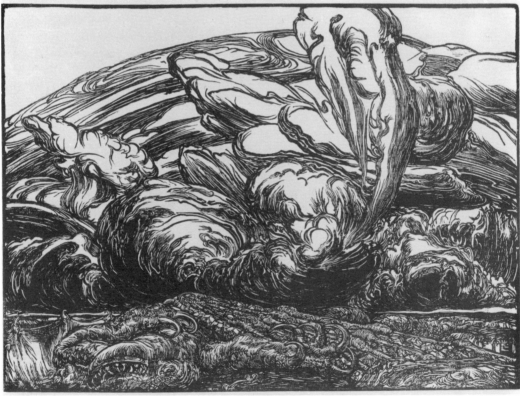

The work of the Vale Press, and three books which preceded its foundation, are best seen against this background of English and French taste. Ricketts and Shannon

Death of the Dragon, woodcut by Thomas Sturge Moore for *The Dial*, no. 4, 1896.

'The Wedding Feast of Daphnis & Chloe' from *Daphnis & Chloe*, 1893. This is the right-hand page of a double-page illustration featuring Ricketts and his friends as guests at the wedding. From left to right: Ricketts, Shannon, Sturge Moore, Lucien Pissarro, Reginald Savage, a 'Mr Riley' sitting opposite Charles Holmes.

Left:
Another woodcut by Edward Calvert. Both were published in an article by Ricketts on woodcuts which appeared in *The Pageant*, 1897.

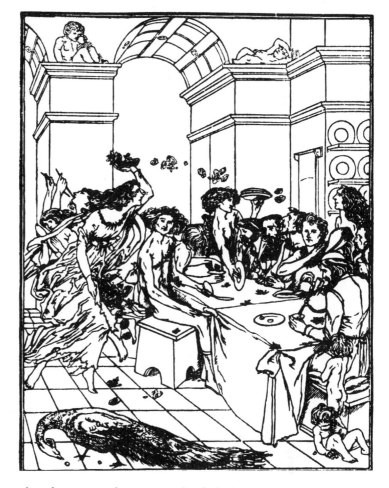

aimed at complete control of design and production on their books and intended to do their own cutting of letters and illustrations. In fact, early illustrations were designed by both of them and redrawn by Ricketts to achieve a uniform effect. Rothenstein described work on the first book, which took eleven months in 1892 and 1893, 'Both he and Ricketts were then busy cutting woodblocks for their edition of *Daphnis and Chloe*, working late into the night, and rising late in the day. Bending over their blocks they looked like figures from a missal. I had never come into touch with the Morris movement, and this craftmanship side was new to me. I was therefore the more impressed by their skill and patience.' One of the designs, the wedding feast, is a portrait group comprising Ricketts and Shannon with Sturge Moore, Lucien Pissarro, Reginald Savage, and a Mr Riley, who did some business for the artists, sitting opposite 'an unfamiliar Holmes', whose appearance Holmes explains: 'As Ricketts sat at work among us one evening, some remark made him rock with laughter, and I heard him say, "Oh damn! I've run the graver

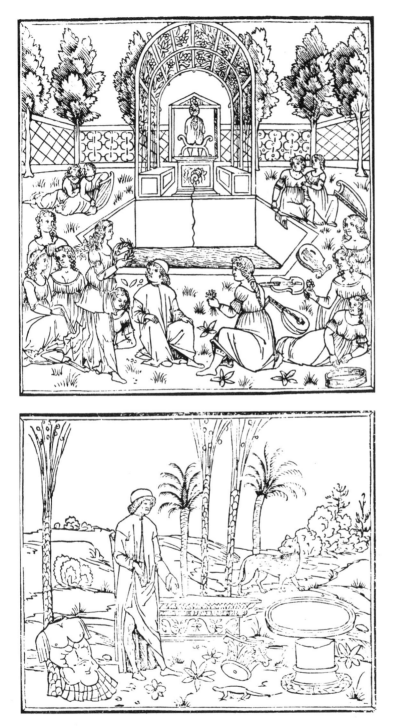

through Holmes's moustache. It must come out.'' And out
it came.' Inspiration for the design of this book was drawn
from the *Hypnerotomachia Poliphili* (The Dream of Poliphi-
lus), published by Aldus in Venice in 1499, rediscovered
in the 1870s, and reproduced in an English facsimile edition

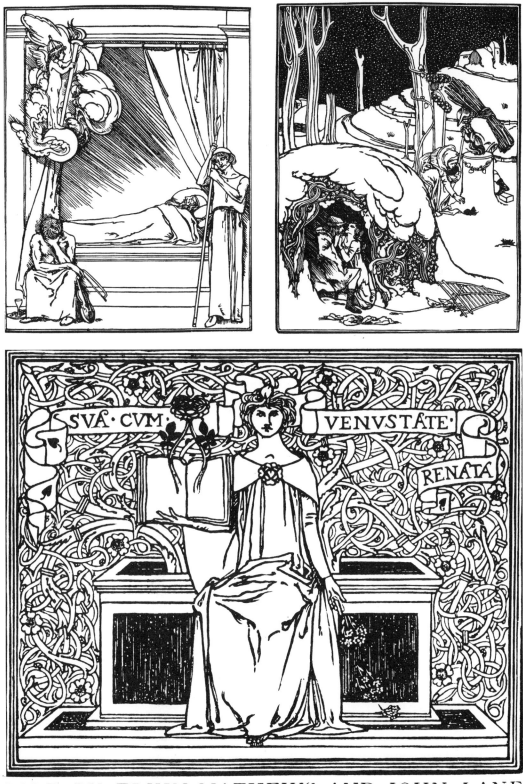

SOLD BY ELKIN MATHEWS AND JOHN LANE

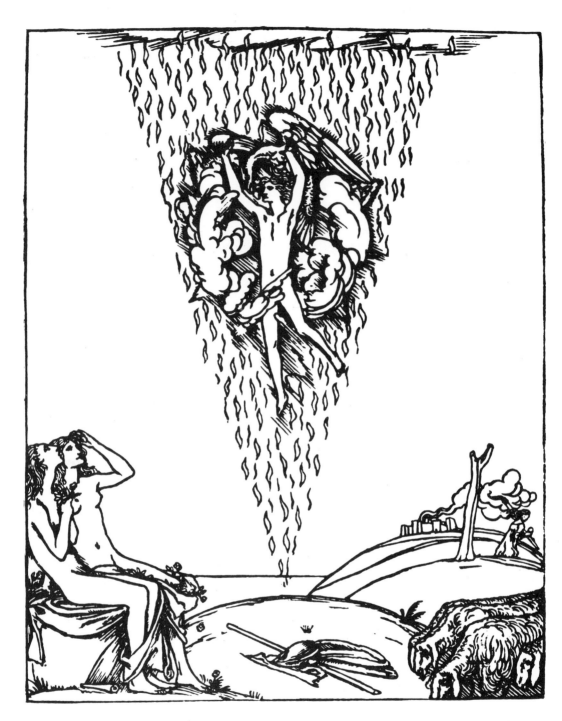

in 1888. The many features of the Italian book which recur in *Daphnis and Chloe* include grotesque decorations, figures after the antique, enigmatic landscapes or architectural backgrounds, and harmony of text with illustration.

The artists' second project was an edition of *Hero and Leander* (1894). Here, the figures are in a style close to that

Illustration for *Daphnis & Chloe* of which 210 copies were printed.

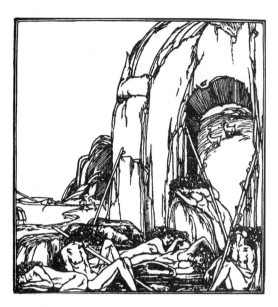

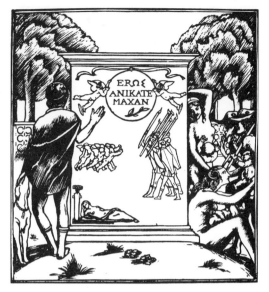

Illustrations for *Daphnis & Chloe*

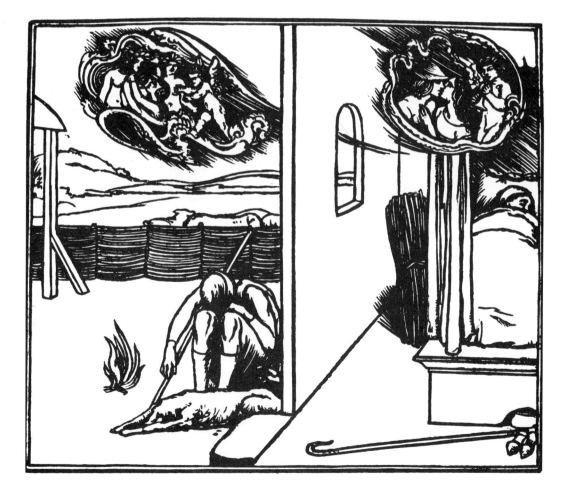

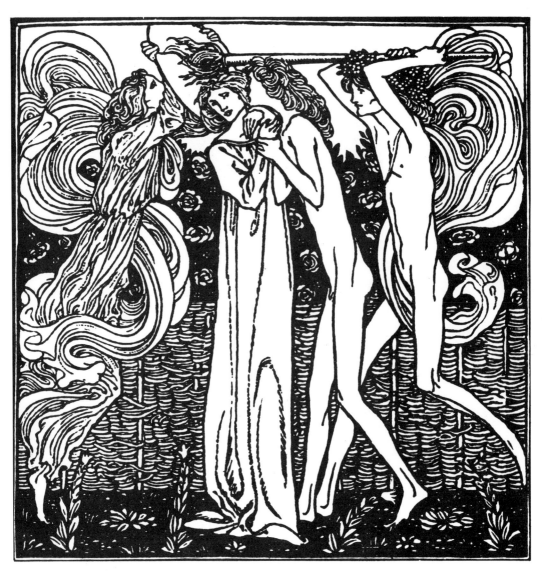

of Rossetti, for they are elongated and crowned with flowing hair, while the swirling forms of water are the emerging shapes of Art Nouveau. The refinements of such illustrations were not readily appreciated, as Ricketts knew. 'In the handling of pictures, the rendering of flesh, hands, feet and faces an original engraver has that chance of refining upon his design, that with an interpreter however skilful cannot be relied on, and that cannot exist at all in process work, however perfect.' His point makes an instructive contrast with Beardsley, a master for process.

Beardsley is often taken as the only typical illustrator of the 'nineties. Both artists worked for Oscar Wilde. *Salomé* (1893) was illustrated by Beardsley and *The Sphinx* (1894) by Ricketts. Ricketts's decorations are symbols, with the burning rocks, the interwoven foliage and a sphinx crouch-

'Coyness and love strive which hath greater grace' from *Hero & Leander* by Christopher Marlowe and George Chapman (Ballantyne Press: Elkin Mathews & John Lane, 1894). This was the second of the books wholly designed and cut by the artists.

42

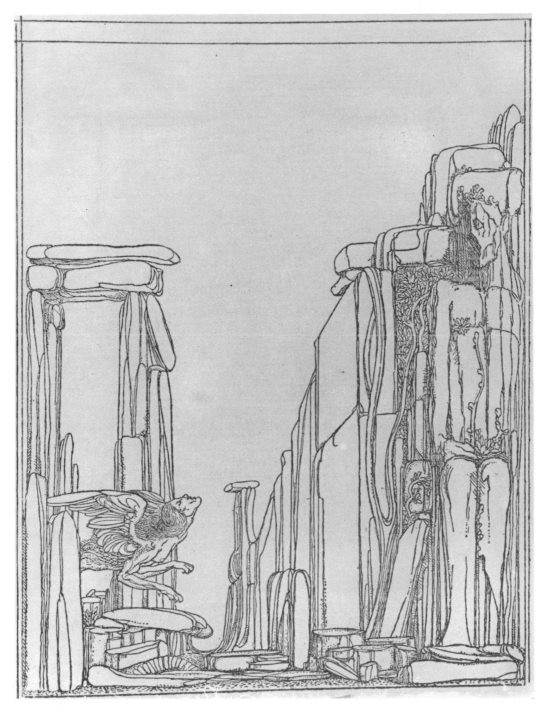

Illustration to *The Sphinx* by Oscar Wilde (Elkin Mathews & John Lane, 1894), a commercial production reproduced from Ricketts' drawings, now unusually rare as most of the edition was destroyed by fire.

ing by a lake. The drawings may have lost in reproduction some of the liveliness achieved by Ricketts and Shannon in their woodcuts; nevertheless *The Sphinx* was designed as a whole by Ricketts and its illustrations match the text. *Salomé* was also reproduced from drawings, but to no disadvantage, since Beardsley was especially adept at drawing

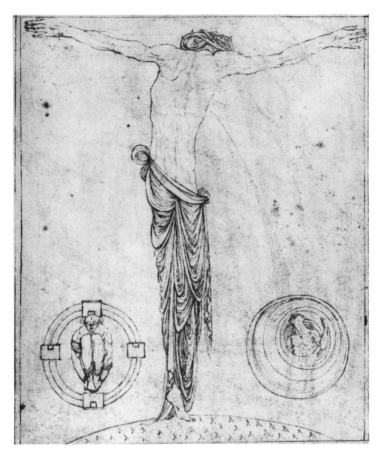

Original pen and ink drawing
Christ Crucified for *The Sphinx*,
bought by William
Rothenstein's brother Charles
Rutherston and now at the City
Art Gallery, Manchester.

exactly for photographic reproduction. His particular limitation was a lack of sympathy for Wilde's text, which he
used as an excuse for clever illustrations like a precocious
schoolboy's drawings, according to the author. The element of satire and shocking sexual allusions or descriptions
in Beardsley's work created a notoriety as well as popular-
ity for his work.

An opportunity then occurred for a business venture,
through Rothenstein's friendship with a lawyer called
Llewellyn Hacon, whom he described as 'a man of the
world, well read and informed on a variety of subjects,
with that special knowledge of the secrets of notables, past
and present, which men of his character possess.'

Hacon agreed at Rothenstein's suggestion to put up
money, with £500 that Ricketts had inherited from his
grandfather, for the establishment of a private press. Ricketts and Shannon made preparation for the press in 1895
and, in the following year, opened a shop in Warwick
Street, engaging a manager, who was replaced by Holmes
in the summer of 1896. Though the printing was to be done
by the Ballantyne Press, the books were to be designed
from cover to cover by Ricketts. The Vale Press was a

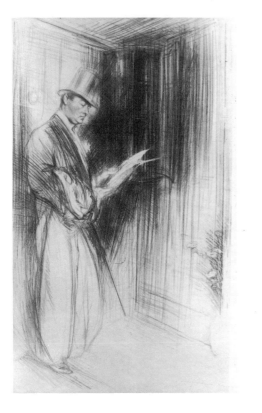

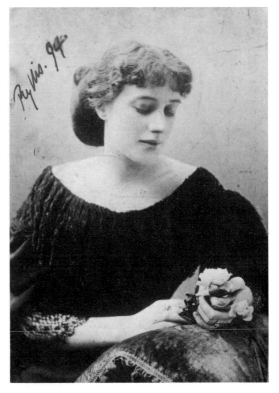

financial and artistic success, as the number and quality of the books listed in its bibliography can testify.

The inspiration for setting up the Vale Press was William Morris's Kelmscott Press, founded in 1891. Two years before, at an important time in the history of the private press movement, Emery Walker had delivered a lecture to the Arts and Crafts Society, based on ideas which he had discussed with Morris. Both men put their ideas into practise, Morris fairly soon in the Kelmscott Press, and Emery Walker more notably in 1900, when he advised Cobden Sanderson at the Doves Press. The ideal of both men was that 'Granted well-designed type, due placing of the lines and words, and the perfect position of the page on the paper, all books might be at least comely and well looking; and if to their good qualities were added really beautiful ornament and pictures, printed books might again illustrate to the full satisfaction of our society that a work of utility might also be a work of art, if we cared to make it so.' Ricketts understood the special artistic character of the Kelmscott Press books and wrote in the bibliography of Vale Press publications: 'A work of art is a whole in which each portion is exquisite in itself, yet co-ordinate.'

During the 1890s, Ricketts and Shannon had many connections with the private presses. Sturge Moore, who edited Vale Press books, also wrote the bibliography for Lucien

Pissarro's Eragny Press. Sydney Cockerell, one of Morris's assistants, wrote about the Kelmscott Press books, besides going on in later life to be associated with the Golden Cockerell Press. The Book Beautiful became an international phenomenon, for in the 'nineties and the early years of the twentieth century the 250 and 350 copies of a special edition often of a classic, necessary for financial success could be sold relatively easily.

Morris had designed three founts for the Kelmscott Press, and Ricketts designed the same number for the Vale Press. The rules of letter design, as Ricketts saw them, were that the characters should be translated from script or chiselled letters to forms which would be natural to metal. His historical knowledge enabled him to look for suitable examples, which he selected irrespective of period. The letter forms of founts are derived first from the fifteenth-century printers, Jenson, and Spira (whom Ricketts particularly admired). His 'Vale' fount was generally well received, although the unusual ampersand and exclamation marks have been criticised. It was the fount most used in the production of Vale books, except for the Vale Shakespeare, for which Ricketts designed the 'Avon' fount. A third was the 'King's' fount, in which the letter forms were derived from Carolingian initials, and the Roman letters of the Renaissance partly avoided. Ricketts at first admitted his preference for it, like a fond father. It looked well, he felt, in Latin. However it was difficult to read, since he had abandoned the tail of the 'g' (a scribe's trick according to Ricketts) and used a Greek 'e', a question mark like an exclamation, and a capital like 'R' in lower case. The rounded forms of 'a', 'e', 'c' and 'b' are attractive. Generally, although the King's fount was little used in Vale Press books, it does not deserve the harsh judgement recorded by Ricketts in his journal as being 'viewed by all as execrable.'

These types are used to good effect in Vale Press books. They are set off with generous spacing – the same medieval manuscript proportions that Morris used for Kelmscott books – and printing inks are varied, so that red or, more rarely, blue or green is sometimes used with black press work. The Vale fount was also used for fourteen books by Lucien Pissarro in the early days of the Eragny Press, before the cutting of his own Brook fount. Vale Press books contain some printers' devices, such as leaf forms, but the main reputation of the press rests on the woodcut initials, borders and illustrative woodcuts. The destruction of more than five years' work on these blocks in a fire at the Ballantyne Press in 1899 made the eventual closure of the Vale Press inevitable by preventing any further use of the early material.

This page, an example of the Vale fount, appearing in *A Bibliography of Books published by Hacon & Ricketts*, 1904.

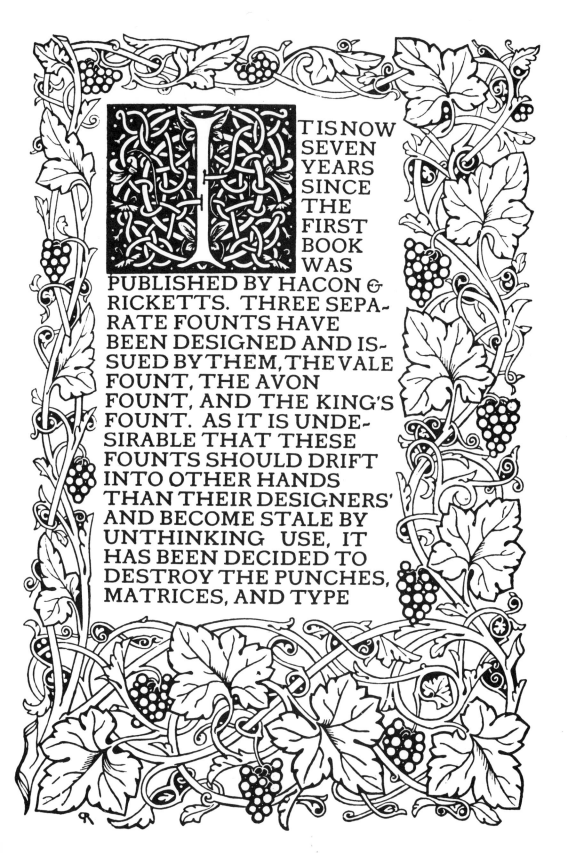

IT IS NOW SEVEN YEARS SINCE THE FIRST BOOK WAS PUBLISHED BY HACON & RICKETTS. THREE SEPARATE FOUNTS HAVE BEEN DESIGNED AND ISSUED BY THEM, THE VALE FOUNT, THE AVON FOUNT, AND THE KING'S FOUNT. AS IT IS UNDESIRABLE THAT THESE FOUNTS SHOULD DRIFT INTO OTHER HANDS THAN THEIR DESIGNERS' AND BECOME STALE BY UNTHINKING USE, IT HAS BEEN DECIDED TO DESTROY THE PUNCHES, MATRICES, AND TYPE

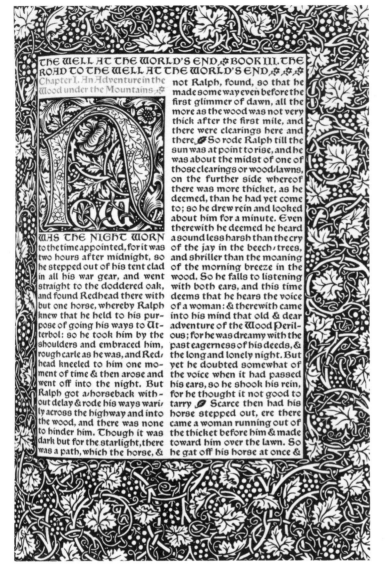

Left & right: Edward Burne Jones' initial and border for *The Well at the World's End* by William Morris (Kelmscott Press, 1896) 'full of wine', is here seen against a Vale Press border 'full of light' from *De Cupidinis et Psyches Amoribus,*1901.

The woodcut initials, though fine, call for no particular comment. However, the border decorations are in a class apart. Holmes rightly judged that Ricketts was unrivalled in his design of woodcut borders; his inventive, intricate patterns succeed with several different motifs, whether vine-leaves and grapes, wild bryony, hops, or knot work derived from Celtic illumination. The borders used by Morris in Kelmscott books, had a dense quality 'as if full of wine', which Ricketts did not wish to emulate, though he admired it. His own aim was to equal books of the Italian Renaissance, which appeared 'full of light'. The differences between their artistic aims have struck critics in different ways, but one obvious contrast is between the sorts of text chosen by the two designers. Morris was drawn

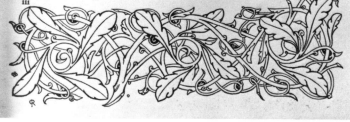

ERANT in quadam ciuitate rex et regina. hi tres numero filias forma conspicuas habuere, sed maiores quidem natu quamuis gratissima specie, idonee tamen celebrari posse laudibus humanis credebantur, at uero puellae iunioris tam praecipua tam praeclara pulchritudo nec exprimi ac ne sufficienter quidem laudari sermonis humani penuria poterat. multi denique ciuium et aduenae copiosi, quos eximii spectaculi rumor studiosa celebritate congregabat, inaccessae formonsitatis admiratione stupidi et admouentes oribus suis dexteram primore digito in erectum pollicem residente, ut ipsam prorsus deam Venerem religiosis adorationibus uenerabantur. iamque proximas ciuitates et attiguas regiones fama peruaserat deam, quam caerulum profundum pelagi peperit et ros spumantium fluctuum educauit, iam numinis sui passim tributa uenia in mediis conuersari populi coetibus, uel certe rursum nouo caelestium stellarum germine, non maria sed terras Venerem aliam uirginali flore praeditam pullulasse. sic immensum procedit in dies opinio, sic insulas iam proximas et terrae plusculum prouinciasque plurimas fama porrecta peruagatur. iam multi mortalium longis itineribus atque altissimi maris meatibus ad saeculi specimen gloriosum confluebant. Paphon nemo, Cnidon nemo, ac ne ipsa quidem Cythera ad conspectum deae Veneris nauigabant. sacra diae praetereuntur, templa deformantur, puluinaria spernuntur, caerimoniae negleguntur, incoronata simulacra et arae uiduae frigido cinere foedatae. puellae supplicatur et in humanis uultibus deae tantae numina placantur, et in matutino progressu uirginis uictimis et epulis Veneris absentis nomen propitiatur, iamque per plateas commeantem populi frequenter floribus sertis et solutis adprecantur.

Haec honorum caelestium ad puellae mortalis cultum inmodica translatio uerae Veneris uehementer incendit animos, et inpatiens indignationis capite quassanti fremens altius sic secum disserit, 'en rerum naturae prisca parens, en elementorum origo initialis, en orbis totius alma Venus, quae cum mortali puella partiario maiestatis honore tractor, et nomen meum caelo conditum terrenis sordibus profanatur! nimirum communi numinis piamento uicariae uenerationis incertum sustinebo, et imaginem meam circumferet puella moritura. frustra me pastor ille, cuius

iii

to romance, taking the Middle Ages as a point of reference. The Vale Press Books were mainly English classics dating from the late sixteenth century onwards – Suckling, Drayton, Campion, Sir Philip Sidney, Blake, Shelley, Robert and Elizabeth Barrett Browning, Coleridge, Arnold and Rossetti. So far as contemporary work was concerned, exceptions were made for Sturge Moore and Michael Field. Decorative borders in sympathy with such authors would inevitably be different from the treatment needed by Caxton's editions of the history of Troy or Beowulf.

The style of wood engraving in Vale Press books was intentionally archaic, for the technical standard of reproductive wood engraving was in general very advanced by

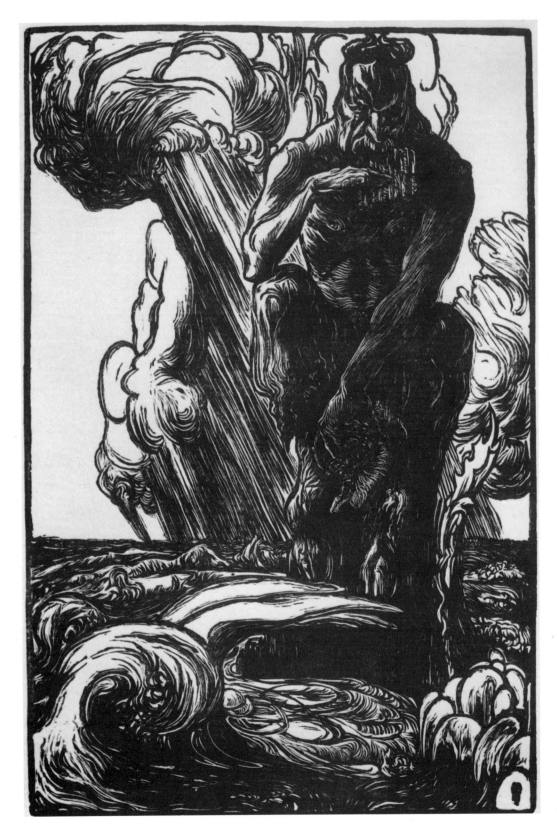

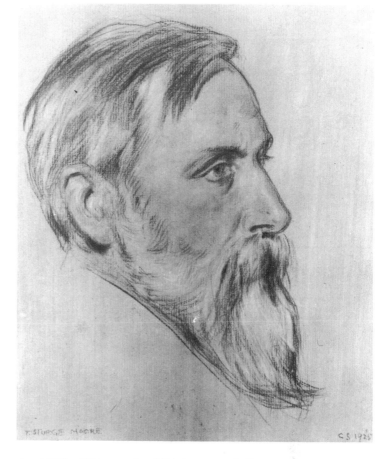

A drawing of Thomas Sturge Moore by Shannon, 1925.

the 1890s. The work of Ricketts and Shannon was distinctive for their use of black line (that is, the engraving of wood blocks so that only the line that is to be printed stands out). It was not the method used in reproduction by the skilled engravers of the period, who practised extensively in white line – the parallel hatchings in Doré's book illustrations, for example, were produced by a whole set of fine gravers, numbered by skilled workmen from 1 to 10 in order of width.

In praising Sturge Moore's work in 1897, Ricketts wrote:

'I would point out that the style of original wood engraving is not here merely accidental, as of a trade engraver who is artist at his leisure, but in aim they show that directness of all work understood within the peculiar conditions of a medium. They aim at effect brought about by white cutting into black, or by black lines showing the work of the tool in their shaping, and we have here no imitation of chalk or wash drawing, or of steel engraving, or of photography.'

Woodcuts for Vale books were designed and cut by the artists and Sturge Moore, while borders were in some cases

A woodcut by Thomas Sturge Moore.

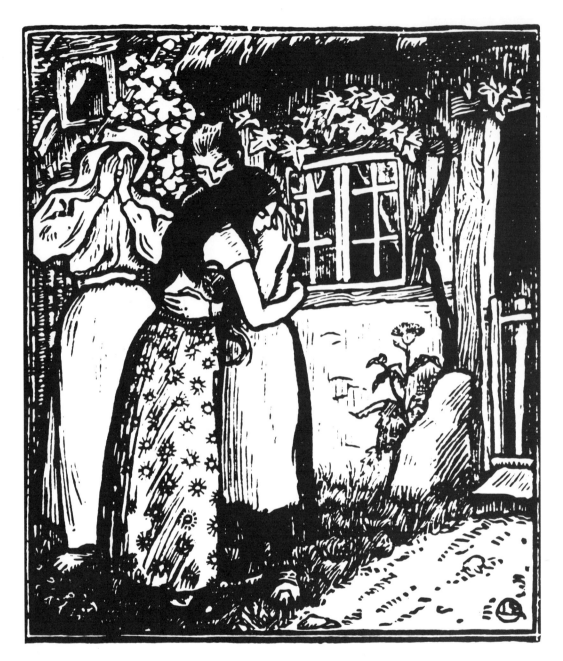

cut by others, notably C. Keats. Comparably original woodcuts were those done by Lucien Pissarro, some as separate pictures, and some as illustrations for his Eragny Press books.

Lucien Pissarro's connection with the artists deserves separate consideration. It was the practice of wood-engraving that they had in common, and their ideas about book design were close enough for Ricketts and Pissarro to write together on the subject. Lucien Pissarro came to

Above & right: Two woodcuts by Lucien Pissarro for *The Dial.* Lucien Pissarro's original and fresh designs fitted well into *The Dial*'s policies.

52

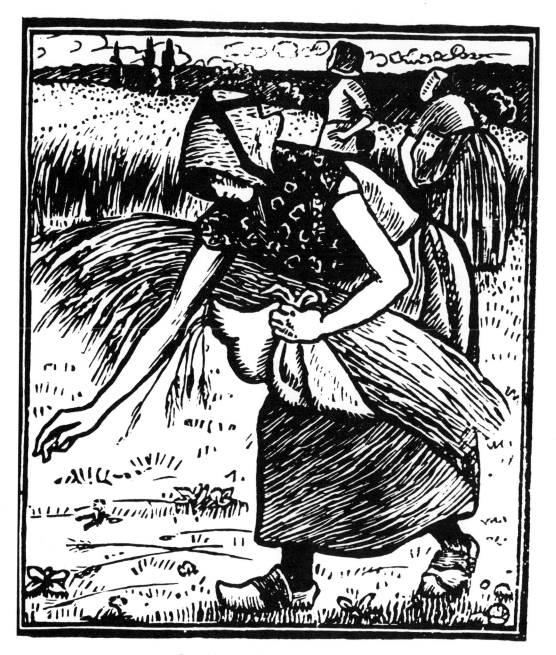

London at the beginning of the 'nineties and married at
Richmond in 1892; Ricketts, Shannon and his father Camille Pissarro were among those at the wedding. Camille
Pissarro was a dominant influence on his son's life, making
sacrifices to enable him to follow an artistic career, active
in advising him, and prepared to assist in projects. Father
and son collaborated in an edition of *Daphnis and Chloe*, for
which Camille Pissarro agreed to make illustrations for engraving by Lucien. In one of the illustrations, Ricketts

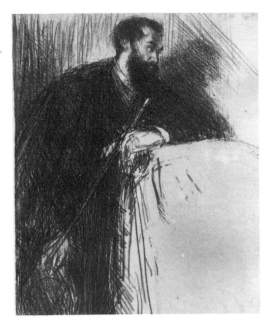

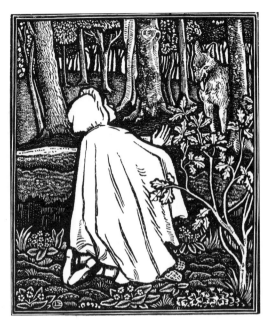

suggested that the figure of Chloe ought to be nude not clothed; Camille Pissarro agreed and redrew the design. Good relations at the beginning of the decade were fostered by the interest that the two English artists took in Camille Pissarro's prints, for which there was at that time no Parisian market. However, differences in their ideas of beautiful books soon emerged. Camille Pissarro saw in books the possibility of fine art, as valid in its own way as a painting, while Ricketts and Shannon regarded books as a branch of design. The contrast expressed itself in more detail with Pissarro's Eragny Press books – on the question of colour printing for example. Their liberal use of time and resources in turn made Eragny Press books more expensive, and the joint marketing of books from the two presses caused difficulties.

In 1894 the artists moved house from The Vale to Beaufort Street where their visitors included Legros, Charles Conder, D. S. MacColl, Roger Fry, and Max Beerbohm, while William Rothenstein called frequently. The first years of the Vale Press had been a time of activity and progress.

Lucien Pissarro gradually withdrew from the close friendship he had shared with Ricketts and Shannon at the beginning of the decade. The extent of the gulf between them is clear from a comment made by Pissarro in 1899 after a visit to a Burne-Jones exhibition, which he described as literature, hardly painting. When he criticised Ricketts's paintings for the same reason three years later his father replied that Ricketts was not a painter but a story teller. Camille Pissaro was not in sympathy with the scholarly

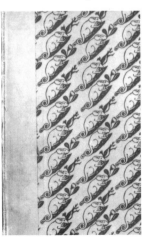

approach of Ricketts and Shannon, and wrote in one letter, 'There is no point in repainting the old masters, however skilfully you do it.' By that time Ricketts had turned away from his former favourable assessment of Impressionism.

When the artists moved from Beaufort Street, they looked for a house in Highgate, but finally settled on Richmond. It was a successful choice, and they spent four happy years there, not out of touch with London life but not too closely involved, as they had felt themselves becoming. In Richmond they took stock; Shannon was able to give shape to his work as a painter, Ricketts had time to develop his interests. During breaks from their work they went bicycling – Shannon was keen enough to go on small tours, usually with Sturge Moore – or on trips on the river, when on at least one occasion they took out May Morris, William Morris's daughter. Their friends Katherine Bradley and Edith Cooper came to live in Richmond. After energetic London days, certainly among the avant garde at the start of the decade, the Richmond years were peaceful – recorded in Ricketts's diary as the happiest in his life.

Ricketts and Shannon had not been to Italy before 1899, although later they travelled a good deal. Their reputations as artists grew gradually, their social contacts extended, and their early years were left behind. Moving from Richmond made a break with the past, and their youth was over.

The Drawing Room at 8, Spring Terrace, Richmond *c*1900.

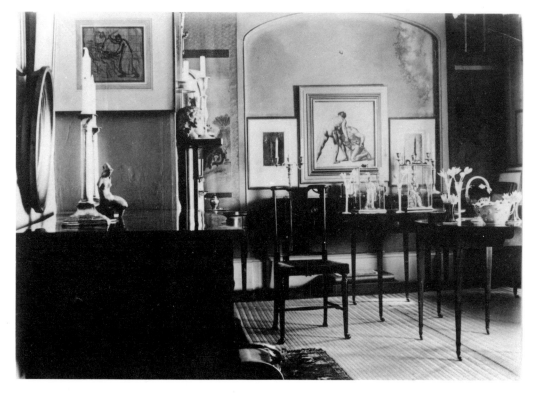

Designs
and Materials

By the turn of the century, Ricketts and Shannon were slowly becoming more successful. A £400 commission to paint portraits of the Dowdall family represented a financial breakthrough for Shannon, while Ricketts's main venture, the Vale Press, achieved a turnover estimated, when it closed, at £36,000. At this time the artists were lucky in winning the friendship and patronage of Sir Edmund Davis, a rich man with mining interests in South Africa. Davis's offer to build studios for them took them from their Richmond retreat to Holland Park, not far from Davis's house, in 1902.

The painters developed an easy friendship with the Davis's; they were invited to dinner, made up parties to the threatre, and were driven in Davis's car to see the coronation procession. Their life was made more comfortable by the roomy, well-designed apartment, which they enhanced with such purchases as satinwood tables and antique mantelpieces, achieving an effect which was grand, yet austere. Shannon's family visited them there and were most impressed.

Since 1898, their enjoyable life in Richmond had enabled the artists to escape from the social and art-political life that had previously occupied so much of their time. Shannon's diaries for those years show that of the twenty or thirty paintings he had in hand he steadily completed commissioned portraits, working on the others as he felt inclined. That pattern continued on his return to London. Davis's friends and acquaintances were a new source of patronage for his work, and the activity of E. J. van Wisselingh, a dealer who ran the Dutch Gallery, kept Shannon's work available to buyers.

The artists' progress was marked by public purchases, including a set of Shannon's lithographs for Dresden, a painting for Bremen, and one of Ricketts's paintings bought by Manchester. Joint exhibitions of their work were held at the Manchester City Art Gallery in 1909 and in New York in 1914. Ricketts wrote that, in the New York show, their work was felt to be ' . . . in the wane of English Victorianism. The last accusation does not pain us. It is

Right: Lansdowne House, Holland Park. The building provided studios for six artists who were commemorated by a plaque in 1979. Besides Ricketts and Shannon, these were their successors Glyn Philpot and Vivian Forbes, F. Cayley Robinson and James Pryde.

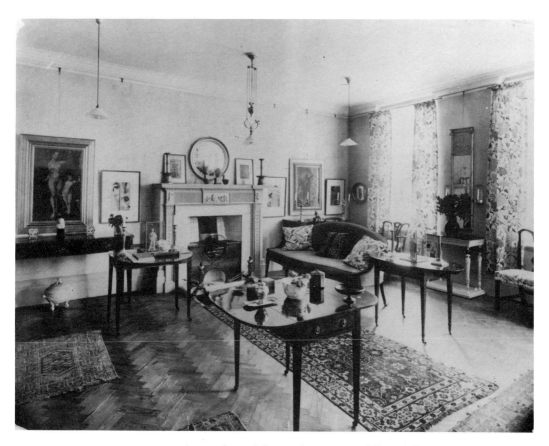

The Lansdowne House
Drawing Room *c*1907.

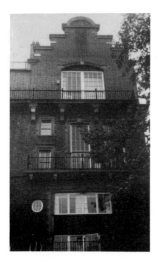

also softened by strictures on Watts, Rossetti and Burne-Jones with whom we are classed – as not reflecting the life of our time.'

The two artists were prepared to defend their policy of remaining aloof from 'common currents and popular aims' more readily because their points of reference were not those of the twentieth century. In his practice as a painter, Shannon followed the example of Watts, a sensitive portraitist and a reflective composer of figure subjects. Ricketts was thought by some friends to have modelled himself on Rossetti and, certainly, a strain of Rossetti's idealism is expressed in Rickett's paintings. Both artists were persistent and careful students of the old masters. According to Shannon's diary a typical week in the Richmond days would have included one or two trips to London on visits to the National Gallery. Essentially, the two men aimed to preserve traditional values.

Ricketts was conscious of their limitations: 'The general strength of our work is in its design, in a regard for our material and I believe in a certain decency of standard in aim. That we may falter in the use of these gifts and remain too attached to tradition I am willing to admit. The ultimate estimate of our work will be made on its success

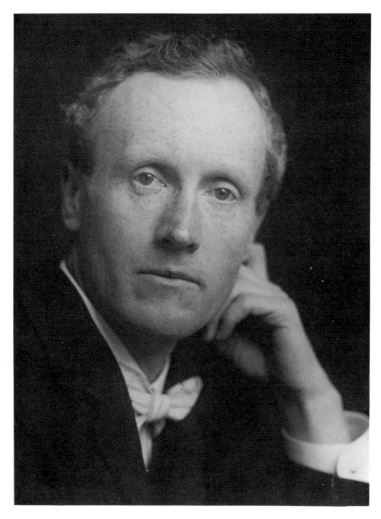

alone. It will be valued not for its originality but for its success.'

Their evident feeling for tradition is a help in our appreciation of the artists' work. Both painted in what they called 'dark keys'. In 1900 Ricketts wrote: 'Discussing the qualities of dark and blond keys in painting with Shannon. We both agree that each is a convention, each being equally arbitrary. In the dark keys lie infinite possibilities of gradation, mystery and suggestion; infinite resources in the mere quality and consistency of the pigments. In the blond keys are possibilities of colour invention and the rendering of form. In the dark keys the oily medium tends to make the picture turgid under revision, the blond keys tend to baldness and lack of quality. All really fine painting – painters' painting – has leant towards the dark keys, from Van Eyck even to Rembrandt. The masterpieces of blond painting exist in fresco and tempera. Their quality is not due to their surfaces but to their designs, or their decorative

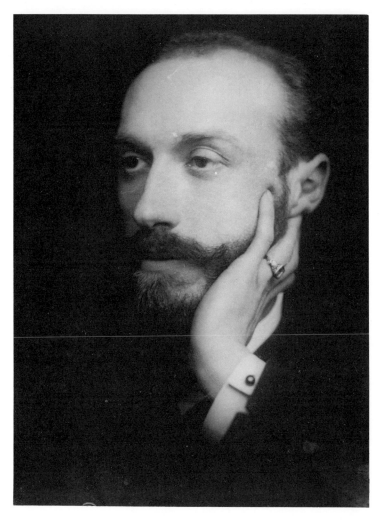

quality. In the blond keys colours can chaunt and clash together; they begin to pulse, vibrate and sing like a musical instrument in the darker method, as with the Venetians whose general pitch is dark.'

The practical application of these ideas is clearly demonstrated in two paintings, Ricketts's *Betrayal of Christ*, one of his best pictures, and *Tibullus in the House of Delia* by Shannon. The meeting with Judas Iscariot is a drama intensified by the figures' gestures; Christ half turns away from the encounter. Ricketts creates a strange atmosphere suffused by evening light. The figures are sombre, the soldiers' torches aflame. The artist is searching for unusual effects. In contrast, Shannon's beautiful *Tibullus in the House of Delia* is more frankly decorative. Both completed within the first five years of the twentieth century, the two pictures reveal the tentative nature of Ricketts's early painting and Shannon's assurance at the same time. *Tibullus* lacks psychological intensity; the theme is bland, with figures

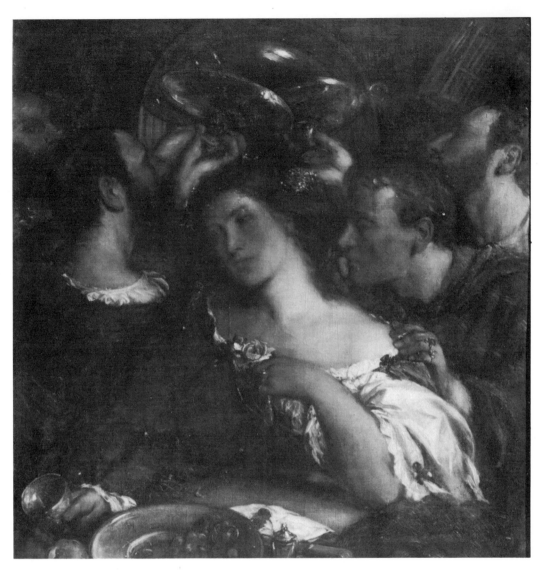

that have no relationship to each other in a narrative or dramatic sense. Portraits of Ricketts and Shannon in the picture revive an old master's custom of the painter including himself and friends. The central figure recalls a woman painted by Rossetti, but the overall design is more reminiscent of Titian or, equally, Rubens. Both the paintings are in the dark key, however.

Among the formative influences on Shannon's art was the work of Velasquez, despite limitations in his knowledge resulting from the small number of paintings in English collections. The spread of the Velasquez cult from France had been helped by Whistler. This was incidentally not the only way in which Whistler was an intermediary for Shannon, since his understated and elegant colours, his example as a lithographer, the portrait compositions and asymmetri-

Above: Tibullus in the House of Delia by Shannon, 1900-05. This is one of two versions in oil which Shannon had previously worked as a lithograph, *In the House of Delia*, 1895, see *right*. Tibullus is shown looking questioningly at Delia to see whether or not she has betrayed him.

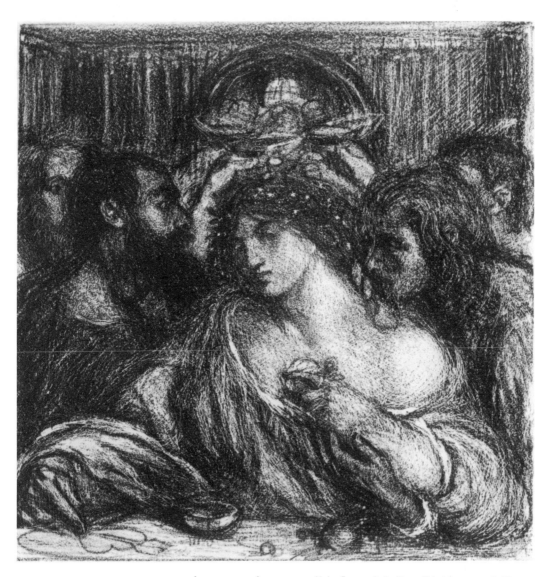

cal typography were all influential. But Ricketts and Shannon made a practice of going to original sources. An idea of Velasquez partly based on reproductions was corrected by Shannon's visit to Madrid in 1900; he reported, 'to my mind he is much flattered by photography.' Although impressed by Velasquez's handling of paint, he was disappointed by the condition of pictures which he thought overcleaned. He felt that Velasquez lacked 'a tender light or source of "colour beauty" ' which could be found in Titian or Rubens.

Although Ricketts and Shannon were not entirely unaware of contemporary developments (they were among the first to recognize Augustus John's talent and bought two drawings while he was still at the Slade School), their approach to technique was far removed from the artistic

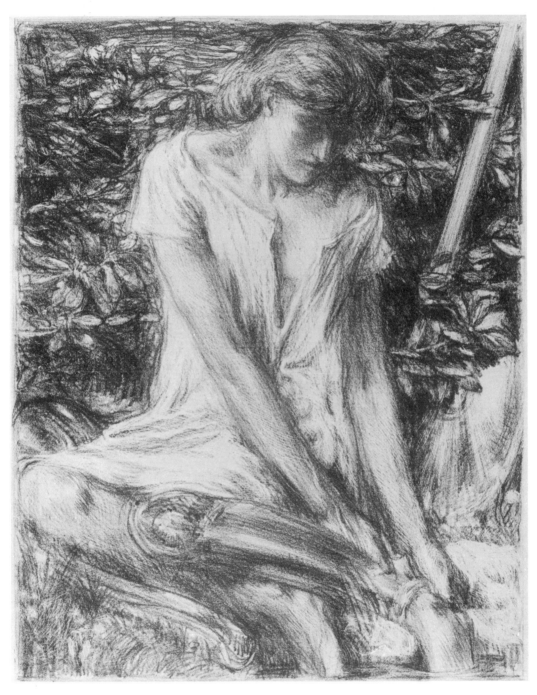

Above: Atlanta, a lithograph by Shannon for *The Dial*, no. 4, 1896.

theories of many contemporaries, whether Impressionists, with their emphasis on the effect of light on subjects, or the new twentieth-century movements, which in different ways renounced traditional values and looked for examples of artistic value in primitive art. Such movements sought to reinterpret the European tradition, not preserve it. Ricketts and Shannon, on the other hand, found it impossible

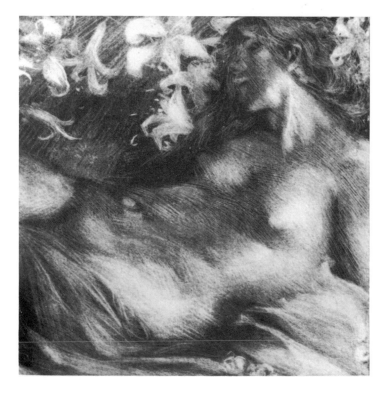

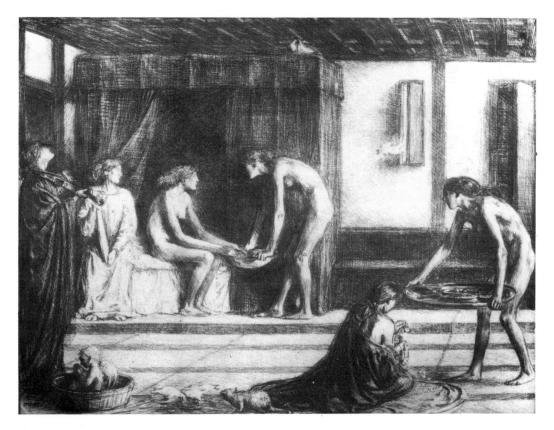

to feel sympathy towards much of the work of their contemporaries. After visiting an exhibition of the New English Art Club in 1904, Ricketts recorded in his diary: 'I thought most of the pictures beastly! It is strange how difficult it is, when one likes good art, to notice bad art, and how difficult it is, when one likes new art, to understand good art.' Technique was not the only point of difference between Ricketts, Shannon and most of their contemporaries – there was also subject matter. Writing about *The Death of Cleopatra*, painted by Ricketts in the tradition of Delacroix, Sickert commented, 'How bewildering your imaginative painter is to us poor realists! . . . Cleopatra . . . and in an age of African luxury, Mr Ricketts makes her luxurious in a box-ottoman without a back. A mere realist would have made Cleopatra a fine woman. However, I am not a critic of imaginative painting, and it is no use talking about things I do not understand. With all this, Mr Ricketts is a pontiff whose lightest word is law. I believe he has already damned impressionism up Notting Hill and down Notting Dale. But we have never damned him.'

The most crucial difference, however, between Ricketts and his fellow artists and critics became clear in 1910, the year in which Virginia Woolf identified a change in the intellectual climate of England, instancing Roger Fry's exhibition of 'Manet and some Post-Impressionists' at the Grafton Galleries. Ricketts reacted fiercely to this show:

'The new ever has to prove its value against the experience of the past before it could be considered admirable. To revert in the name of "Novelty" to the aims of the savage and the child – out of lassitude of the present – is to act as the anarchist, who would destroy where he cannot change. To wish to blot out the page upon which our knowledge is written, in the hope of a new thrill of expectancy, is an old form of petulance. It is as old as the spirit that denies.'

Ricketts thought little of Impressionism, but for Cézanne he had no regard at all. 'Cézanne's paintings are laboured in effect: a suffering sense of "values" made him plaster his canvases with pigment in some sort of parody of the pictures of Manet. For a while he plodded on, affording Zola copy for his novel *L'Oeuvre*. To Manet and Degas he seemed but a provincial satellite, a compromising follower of Impressionism. He left Paris doubtful of himself, doubtful also of the school whose novelty and notoriety had cast a spell on him. He is one of those countless failures who have set out "to conquer Paris", to use the romantic phrase of M. Zola's.' Ricketts wrote less bitterly of Gauguin's work: 'Dare I confess that I do not always dislike his pictures of Tahitian life. Their technical shortcomings have a left-handed affinity with Degas's later and "less-studied"

Opposite, top left: signboard for The Vale Press at Warwick Street painted by Shannon.

Top right: The Betrayal of Christ by Ricketts, 1904.

Below, top left: 'The Blue Bird' brooch made for Edith Cooper, 1899. Gold and enamel set with semi-precious stones. *Bottom left:* The Sabbatai ring shaped like a Byzantine church in two-colour gold set with cabochon chalcedony with green stone behind the church windows, 1904. The ring was designed to appeal to the five senses with a piece of ambergris inside for the smell and pieces which rattled for sound. *Right:* Gold and enamel pendant set with semi-precious stones designed for 'Amaryllis', Mrs Llewellyn Hacon, in 1900. The pendant was made up to Ricketts' design by Giuliano.

Overleaf: The Shell Gatherers (The Pearl Fishers) painted by Shannon *c*1894-98.

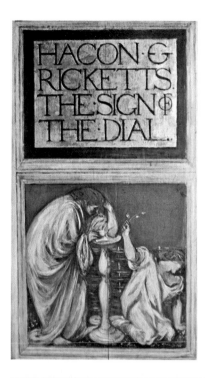

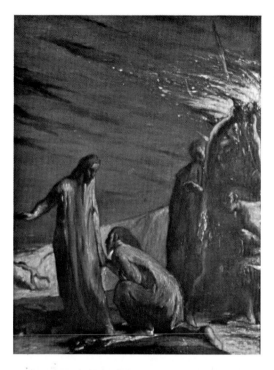

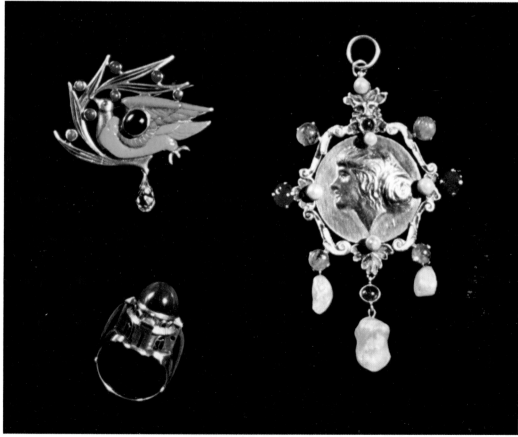

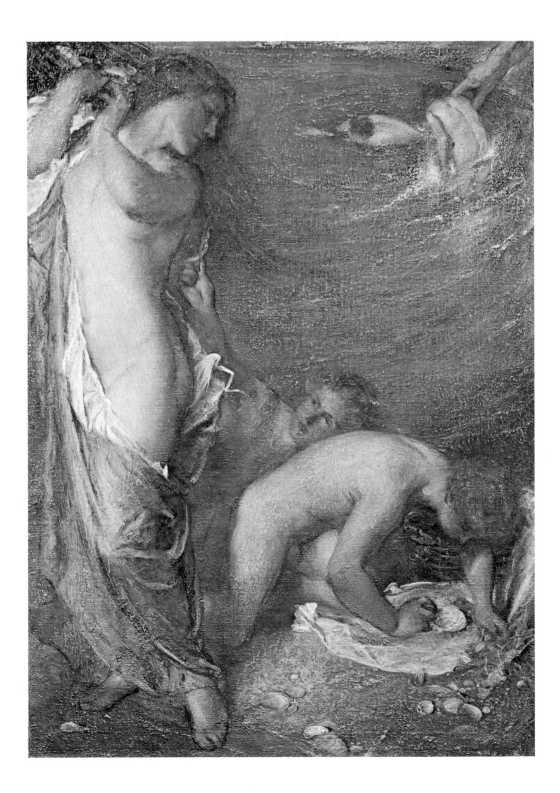

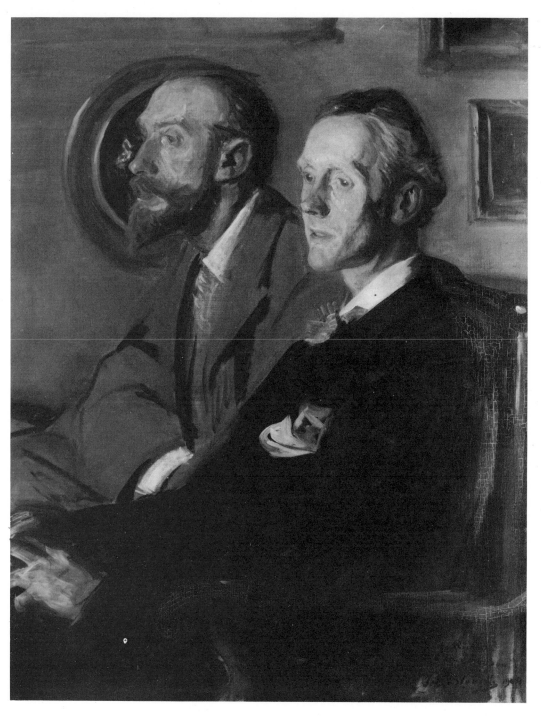

Above: Ricketts and Shannon painted in 1904 by Jacques-Emile Blanche, who described their life as ideal *'Tout pour l'art'*.

works. The strangeness of his subject-matter attracts me, not his painting.' But Van Gogh is dismissed as 'This man who suffered under the stress of religious and artistic mania.' Ricketts's extreme views mark his separation from the emerging modern movement. In 1914 he was to reveal his feelings of his, and Shannon's, isolation:

'Against us are both the last and the present generation of painters and critics, against us is our small output and slow sales ... We both wonder if our next picture will be comparable to our last, sometimes look back with envy upon earlier works. We are, I believe, less self-confident and less self-reliant, which is wrong. Success belongs to belief, and, in our case, a certain diffidence is complicated by distrust in our contemporaries, and we believe that art must undergo a period of disinterest. The wrong thing has been too constantly encouraged, and England lacks the gift of respect which abroad surrounded older eminent men.'

By then, the two artists' aims had been clearly established for more than a decade. Shannon's work showed little change, or development, from the late 1890s, by which time he had already achieved the allusive charm and refined technique which characterise his paintings. The consistency of Shannon's work was partly explained by his exchange of opinions with Ricketts – each artist showed the other his work and acted on the resulting criticism. Shannon's diary shows gratitude for Ricketts's advice and suggestions which dealt, certainly in part, with tonal qualities, since Shannon's technical notes often record the moderation of harsh effects. In 1905 he recounts a rare instance of disagreement over *Tibullus in the House of Delia*, when he felt Ricketts had misunderstood the painting. Unfortunately Shannon's diaries were either not kept up or have not survived after 1906, so that we are unable to follow such interchanges into the 1920s.

Ricketts was clearly delighted with his friend's successes. In 1900 he noted that Shannon's painting stood out like an old master in a singularly lifeless English section at the Universal Exhibition in Paris. A day or two later, he heard that 'Whistler had been vastly struck by C. H. S.'s *Marmiton* picture, returning to it again and again, with the exclamation: "How is it done?".'

Ricketts was perceptive in writing about his friend's paintings, which he saw as much in the context of French art as in the English artistic tradition. For him, the poetry of Shannon's work escaped analysis, although it had the liveliness of a sensitive and recollected spirit (*'un élan d'esprit sensitif et recueilli'*). Ricketts described Shannon's preference in composition for splitting the classical pyramidal form in two, so as to frame the centre of the canvas with figures. A luminous quality in Shannon's pictures was imparted by outlining the main figure in a sober tone against the grey of a wall, or placing the figure prominently against the waves of a purple sea, burnt by the fire of a heavy sun. Ricketts was careful to refer to European standards when praising Shannon's work.

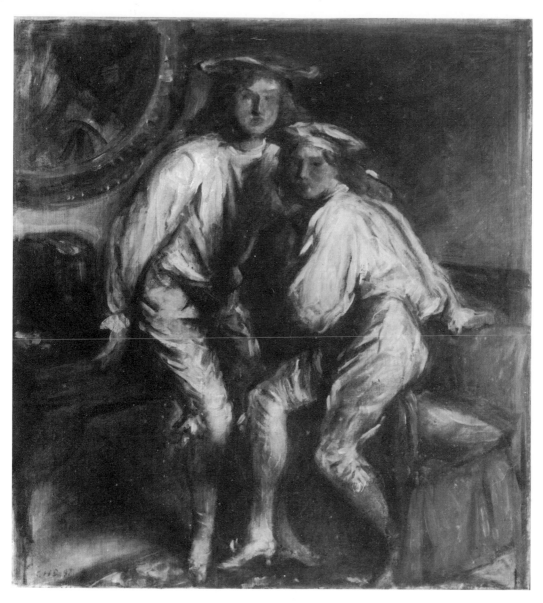

Les Marmitons, 1897. This study
in the Tate Gallery is for
Shannon's major painting
completed in 1899 and
exhibited in Paris at the
Exposition Universelle in 1900.

Shannon's best pictures were idylls. If Watts could be
regarded as England's Michelangelo, then Shannon was
an English Giorgione, as Laurence Binyon described him
in a catalogue of 1907. Among his subjects at the turn of
the century were *The Shell Gatherers*, *A Romantic Landscape*
and *The Golden Age*. For his Royal Academy Diploma picture he chose *Vanity and Sanctity*, figures seated in a garden
setting at Chilham Castle. Compared with others shown at
the Royal Academy in the 1920s, Shannon's pictures are
conspicuous against a background of the well-tried for-
mulae of landscapes, genre and portraiture.

Shannon's portraits are often distinguished and always
refined. His admirable lithographs of friends in the 1890s

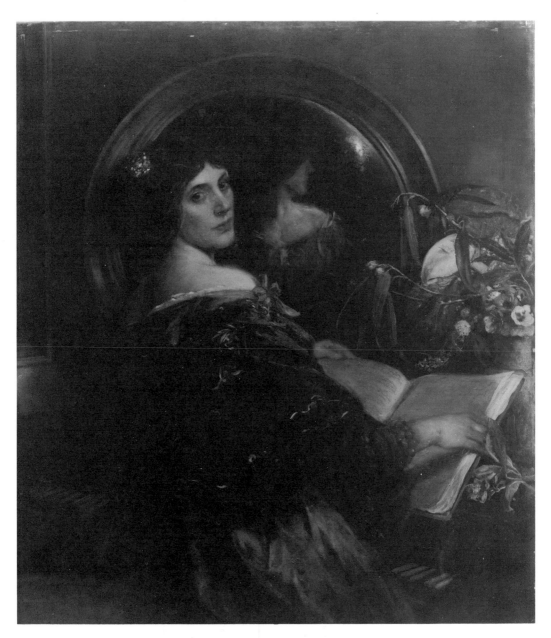

show a sensitive touch which he applied to his portraits of women. Whistler and Legros appreciated the qualities noted in his paintings by Ricketts as a delicacy of tone, a thoughtful elegance and a contemplative charm. He chose simple but effective poses for his self-portrait and a portrait of Ricketts painted at the end of the 1890s, both formerly the property of Sir Edmund Davis and now in the National Portrait Gallery. In later portraits, like Rossetti, he often selected a particular motif to set off a personality, as in *The Lady with the Amethyst* or *The Lady with a Fan*. Unluckily for him, he was from time to time taken for another painter,

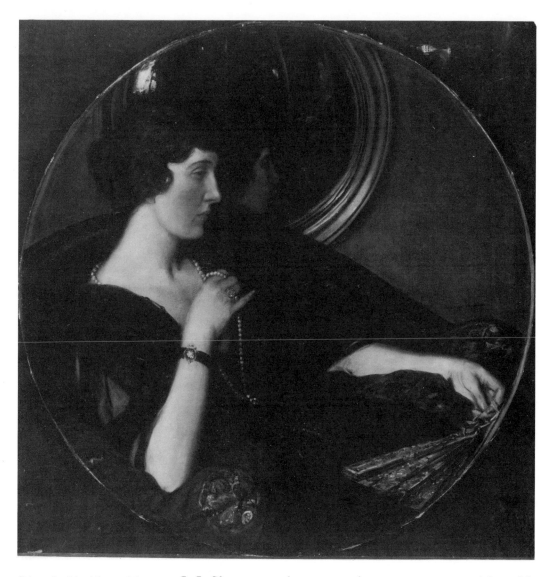

Princess Patricia of Connaught by Shannon, 1917-18.

J. J. Shannon – the most welcome error was a visit to his studio from Princess Patricia of Connaught, who insisted, when she learned of her mistake, that Charles Shannon, too, should paint her portrait. His picture characteristically shows an imaginative trait of interpretation lacking in the more flattering and status-bound picture by Sir James.

In personality, as in their art, where Shannon was calm, Ricketts was restless. When the Vale Press closed, Ricketts had difficulty in finding a direction. His artistic success in the 1890s had been based on the skill in draughtsmanship which led Lord Leighton to commission from him a drawing of *Oedipus and the Sphinx*. The work pleased Leighton with its 'weird charm'. When Ricketts took to painting at the beginning of the century, he received lessons from Shannon. He was not naturally fluent as an oil painter,

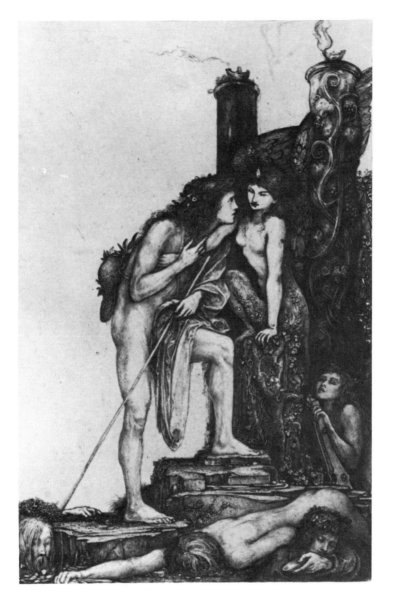

though his pictures are often of great interest as attempts
at visual effects that had rarely been tried before. The
subjects of his pictures had none of the serenity of
Shannon's idylls. Ricketts tended to select such dramatic
themes as *The Good Samaritan* or *Don Juan*, and his pictures
in the Royal Academy shows of the 'twenties included
Chimaerae and *Jepthah's Daughter*. Ricketts sought myths –
as Yeats remarked to him, he painted the tragedy of man.
Looking at his own work in the face of some adverse criticism, Ricketts found himself pleased with the 'sense of
design, the emotions of awe, melancholy and compassion
in my work'. Taking a characteristic theme, the tragedy of
Montezuma, Sturge Moore commented:

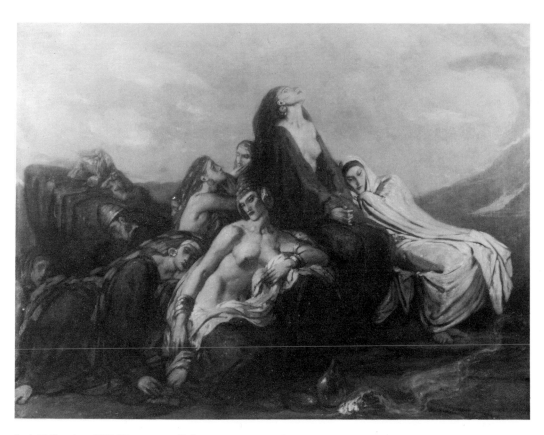

Jepthah's Daughter, *c*1905-07. This picture is based on the Bible story where Jepthah vows to God that, if he is granted victory, he will sacrifice the first thing he sees on his return home – which is his daughter running to greet him. The choice of subject is as typical as Montezuma for Ricketts, and, interestingly, the composition of a standing figure among others reclining or lying is similar.

'My answer need not be yours, but to provoke yours let me remind you of Montezuma's death. Mexico lay at the mercy of the fire-armed Spanish invaders, when their Aztec priest and king, having immolated his people to the sun which had enabled them to live, as the sun set slew himself on the top of the hecatomb. A great conquered nation accepted its overthrow by dying with its god in an act of worship.'

Sturge Moore goes on to say that, for Ricketts, an acceptance of life and a loyalty to experience were crucial. Don Juan, for example, he regarded as 'a profoundly significant figure, a kind of saint. Derider of all attempts to justify God's ways to man, the Don accepted the baseness of men, women, and institutions, and glorified in the power it gave him.' Don Juan's attitude was 'essential to the ideal man – complete mental freedom from conventions and traditions, and an utter loyalty to his own experience.'

Ricketts's paintings are essentially evocations, almost expressions of a philosophy of life. Though a remarkable decorator, Ricketts seemed unable to concentrate his powers in painting. He saw himself as having two personalities,

' . . . the born ornamentalist one finds in the details of my theatre work, and the rather hectic improvisatore of my paintings and bronzes. Both currents run side by side and refuse to blend. My painting refuses to face detail and certain kinds of invention, which Moreau or Burne-Jones have at their finger-tips. Once the pencil or point is in my hands I am incapable of breadth or suggestion and can lapse into an almost Persian finick and finish.'

As a craftsman, he was proficient in a variety of media, but did not include lithography among his successes. There, he was frank about his failure. 'Find the medium, like pastel, unsuited to me. Hence intense depression. There is something disheartening facing an almost certain failure. One can work thirteen hours a day if one's work is steady definite progress, as in wood-engraving.'

Jewellery, on the other hand, was a branch of design that Ricketts enjoyed. He kept stones in a drawer, setting them out as he worked on a design, which he would then send to a professional jeweller to be made up, usually as a wedding present. Giuliano was among the jewellers who had to contend with Ricketts's hopes for elegance in a setting which at times proved incompatible with the technical demands of the craft. Some of his surviving jewels are extremely fragile. On one occasion, he was so dissatisfied with the interpretation of his design that he·gave away the brooch intended as a gift for Laurence Binyon's bride to a model at that moment posing in his studio. His style as a

Below left: A design for a pendant jewel by Ricketts from his album of *Designs for Jewellry (sic) done in Richmond 1899* now in the British Museum.
Right: The Pegasus pendant containing a miniature of Edith Cooper, 1901. When Ricketts had painted the miniature, Katherine Bradley felt that it should have a fine setting. On her death it was presented to the Fitzwilliam Museum from 'Michael Field'.

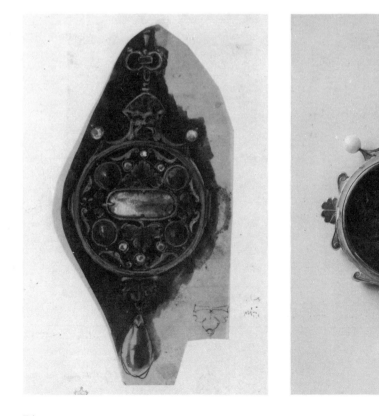

designer of jewellery was eclectic. He gave the miniature he painted of Edith Cooper a setting reminiscent of the Renaissance, while the low-relief portrait on a jewel for Llewellyn Hacon's wife comes closer to Art Nouveau. It was an extravagant hobby which he was persuaded to give up, though Shannon, who influenced his decision, was pleased with a ring made for him with emerald and lapis lazuli set side by side. Jewellery was an artistic sideline which may be seen, with Shannon's design of furniture or a cretonne, as evidence of the artists' versatile gifts.

Another medium that attracted Ricketts was sculpture, familiar to him from his student days in Lambeth, where sculpture was taught and practised, and where foundry work could be carried out. Most of his sculptural work dates from the first decade of the century, although the head of Cecil Lewis, his only portrait, was done in the 1920s. Most typical of his pieces are the small bronzes of which he exhibited twelve in the Carfax Gallery in 1906, including *Orpheus and Eurydice, Sphinx, Paolo and Francesca*

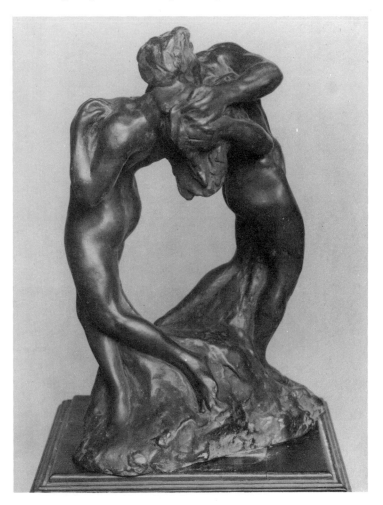

Ricketts' bronze, *Orpheus and Eurydice*. This was sufficiently identifiable as his style for Max Beerbohm to use it in a caricature of the two artists in 1907.

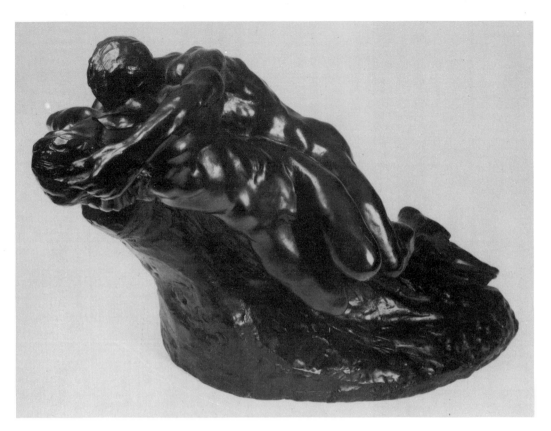

and *Io and the Nymphs*. Ricketts had been inspired by the example of Rodin to embark on sculpture and, although he could never match Rodin's sense of scale and feeling for three-dimensional form, he modelled flesh against flesh, as Rodin did; he also used mythical subjects without giving the figures realistic attributes. Watts and Alfred Stevens were among Ricketts's sources. His gift for outline was noted by the sculptor Henry Poole 'Whatever may be said about that fellow's anatomy, no matter from where you look at his statuettes, you see a telling silhouette, and it is only great masterpieces that rival him in that.' A perceptive but incomplete comment, for not only masterpieces have telling silhouettes, so do the Tanagra figures of which Ricketts and Shannon were keen collectors. Although Ricketts's small bronzes were admired, they did not sell. 'My bronze show has cost me fifty pounds. During the exhibition one bronze sold, value twenty-five pounds, to a friend. My picture show was a failure: one picture sold to Pye, value twenty-five pounds.' This professional disappointment was an important factor in his undertaking to write a book about Titian. But at the same time there were diversions in theatre work, with which he became increasingly involved, so much so that by the 1920s his stage work had become absorbing.

Above: Paolo & Francesca, 1909. Reminiscent of Rodin's modelling of figures, this was in the exhibition at the Carfax Gallery and greatly disappointed Ricketts by not selling.

It is interesting to note a feature of composition that is found in his sculptural work as well as in his paintings. He either places his figures in a close relationship, perhaps huddled together as in *Jepthah's Daughter,* or achieves the tense juxtaposition of *Betrayal of Christ,* and the bronze *Orpheus and Eurydice.* While such compositions heighten the drama of his subjects, they are entirely absent from Shannon's pictures, where figures are invariably in an easier relationship with one another.

The two artists achieved recognition among some of their contemporaries, although not the avant garde, and eventually by election to the Royal Academy. In 1904, say, they both thought of themselves as inevitably excluded from the Academy and exhibited at the International Society, also joining some colleagues in a group of painter-engravers which was to become the Society of Twelve. Their work was shown in Society of Twelve exhibitions and at small galleries like that run by Van Wisselingh or the Carfax Gallery, run at first by John Fothergill and then by Robert Ross (who answered an enquiry about the gallery's finances, 'We just manage to keep our head below water.'). When Shannon was asked in 1905 if he would allow his name to go forward as a candidate for the Royal Academy, he reacted with astonishment and discomfiture. 'We quarrelled all the way home on the subject, I being in favour of allowing things to take their course and decide when the time arrived. Shannon being delirious with his dread of ridicule and the fact that the society was obsolete, and would be ludicrous in a few years, and that Watts had already regretted his R. A. ship. All this is true, but if they move to elect him without effort on his part it counts, and the future is uncertain, after all.' Shannon was elected an Associate in 1911, R. A. in 1920, while Ricketts became an Associate in 1922 and R. A. in 1928.

The pattern of the artists' lives was a comfortable one. In the years before 1914 they made a number of journeys abroad, including a visit to Egypt and Greece in 1911 (to combat Shannon's rheumatism) and a return trip to Egypt in 1912–13. Their London life was socially active; they took an interest in the affairs of the International Society, became involved in the theatre, and attended plays and concerts, particularly enjoying the Russian Ballet seasons. A small circle of close friends saw them, especially on Friday evenings, when they extended an open invitation, a common custom in the 'nineties, on one evening a week. After their return from Richmond, the puzzle of entertaining a wider circle was solved by Shannon's idea of offering afternoon tea; the seventy guests who came to their first tea party made up what Ricketts described as a social salad. Connoisseurs, literary friends, museum officials, theatre

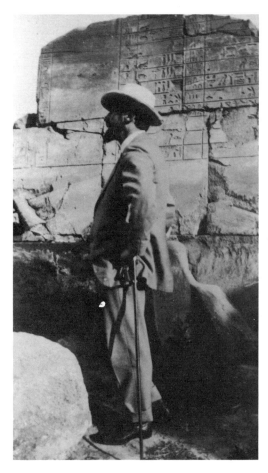
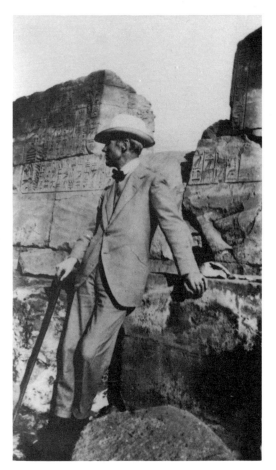

people, musicians, artists and sculptors came and went. For an artist in difficulty, like R. F. Wells, they arranged commissions; to a discovered talent like Ernest Cole they gave encouragement. Looking back over his diaries, Ricketts felt that 1906 had been a year of especial interest: 'Quite interesting people turn up!' In the period before 1914 the two friends were consolidating their reputations as artists and connoisseurs, and dealing on equal terms with, say, Shaw, Diaghilev, or Thomas Beecham.

The war years were difficult for them, although a legacy from Michael Field helped them financially during that period. Like other artists, they were engaged in charity work, and subscribed works of art or possessions to such events as Red Cross sales. Among their friends was Princess Alice of Monaco who gave lunches at Claridges where they were kept aware of the progress of the war and its distressing record of losses among Europe's artistic and cultural treasures. Another acquaintance was Wickham Steed, editor of *The Times*, who also had a flat in Lansdowne House. Ricketts took an active part in some of the public issues of the day, such as ensuring adequate protection for the pic-

Above: Ricketts and Shannon photographed during one of their trips to Egypt.

78

tures in the National Gallery, and bringing to public attention the threat that the British Museum might be appropriated by the Air Board. This success helped to strengthen the good relations that Ricketts had already established with museum officials. In 1915 for example, it was suggested that he should become the Director of the National Gallery, but he declined. It was a decision that he afterwards regretted, and perhaps his theatre work was in some way a distraction from the feeling that he had lost a significant opportunity.

At the end of the war, the two artists were both in their fifties, and they saw rather less of their contemporaries. One contributing factor was that Sir Edmund Davis gave them tenure of the keep at Chilham Castle in Kent, in gratitude for their advice on picture purchases. At the Davis's house parties they met a variety of guests, some of whom, like the young Constant Lambert, made a good impression. While Shannon remained absorbed in his work, Ricketts found time to encourage other people's projects besides engaging in his own. When Ricketts and Shannon gave up their flat to buy a house, it was taken over by two young painters, Glynn Philpot and Vivian Forbes, whom Ricketts would have liked to see as the new Ricketts and Shannon. One of those who benefited from his interest was Cecil Lewis, whom Ricketts encouraged in his ambition as a writer. At a time of some depression for Ricketts,

Right: an interior of the Keep at Chilham Castle while Ricketts and Shannon lived there.

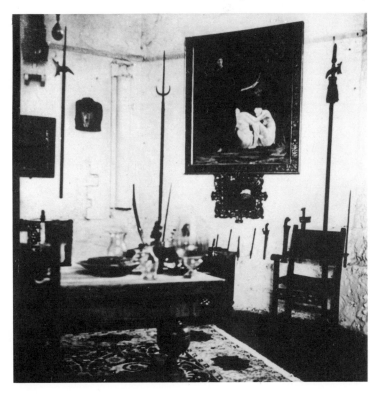

he went with Lewis to Tunisia; similarly in 1929 he went abroad with Henning Nyberg to Italy. Early in that year, the artists' life together had been brought to an end by Shannon's severe fall. He suffered concussion and never recovered his faculties, but lived until 1937; Ricketts died of a heart attack in 1931.

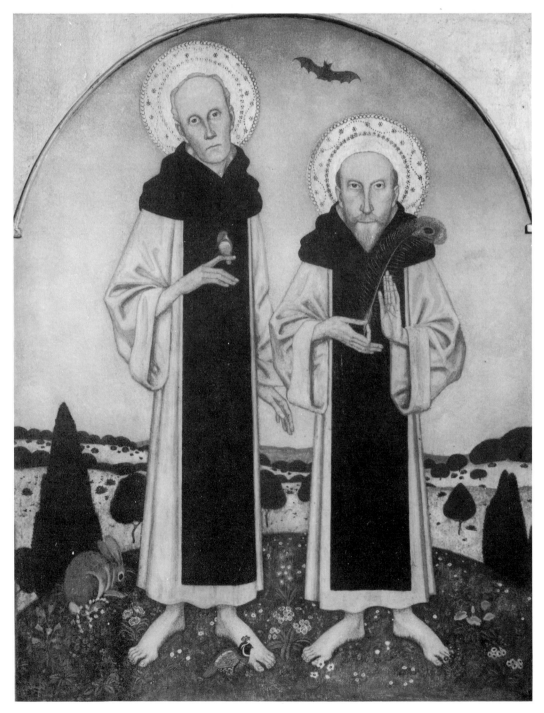

A Bias for Beauty

Ricketts's three books of art criticism, *The Prado and its Masterpieces* (1903), *Titian* (1910) and *Pages on Art* (1913), remain a pleasure to read. Ricketts's talent for conversation that so attracted and influenced his contemporaries, seems to linger ' in certain descriptive phrases or judgements, which clearly convey his enthusiasm for the art he most admired. However, in considering his explicit views on European art set down in these three books, we ought not to forget the influence Ricketts exerted; his knowledge and preferences are implicit in the books and lives of his friends.

Understanding Ricketts's admirable taste as an expression of his personality, Sturge Moore took the nature of that taste (and the manner in which it had been formed) as a model in his own general book on art appreciation, *Armour for Aphrodite*: 'The taste of a Flaubert or a Rossetti, a Baudelaire or an Arnold, a Paul Valéry or a Charles Ricketts, is necessarily limited. The delicacy of the senses, the energy of attention, the courage for acting on experience, will fail here or there in them or in any others whose names may be preferred. Besides, all of them suffer from accumulated hindrances due to the untimeliness of experiences, or a dearth of them, or of freedom to explore them. Yet all of these improved their taste during several more or less continuous spells, and are examples of very rare gifts and acquirements among their contemporaries, and are all pre-eminently men of taste as well as creators.'

In another passage, Sturge Moore gives advice on the need to make personal choices in developing taste, and recalls Ricketts's method: 'Our homes have been so invaded by an abject commercialism which counts pecuniary profit as the one thing necessary, that the craftsman is today always surrounded by hostile and depressing aspects. How can he free himself? I have one suggestion. Let him begin in the corner of one room or garret to order everything according to his taste, to admit nothing into it that does not fascinate his gaze. He can tack or paste brown or white paper over the wall and set an old ginger jar with a branch of spring buds, autumn leaves, or summer flowers, before it, or pin upon it a picture postcard of the work of

Ricketts and Shannon as Medieval Saints by Edmund Dulac. Dulac neatly and affectionately caricatured the two artists in a landscape if not medieval, then perhaps trecento.

'There was a young lady of Annan
Whose father-in-law was a Canon.
    She gave up the church
    For artistic research
And consorted with Ricketts and Shannon.

81

art that he oftenest longs to see – banishing whatever comes to offend him and replacing it by better. The corner may very well end by compromising his whole home and making it his in a new sense that corresponds with his advance in life and the pride that begets. The greatest designer of modern times has in this way come to own the most beautiful rooms in London, and the richest in works of art: yet I can remember when he could rarely afford more than one square meal a week, his other repasts consisting chiefly of bread, jam and tinned meats, though his room was even then beginning to be an astonishment envied by rich men.'

Charles Holmes, too, benefited from Rickett's knowledge in his case concerning technique. With his book *Notes on the Science of Picture-making*, published in 1909, Holmes hoped to make a synthesis of very different viewpoints by concentrating not on abstract principles, but on 'the practical sciences of picture-making, of sculpture-making and the like, and not upon any group of abstract ideas, that the aesthetic philosopher of the future will have to erect the complete all-embracing theory which will enable artists to be peaceable, art patrons to be confident, and art critics to be unanimous.' Holmes knew that his own special aptitude in the appreciation of painting was an understanding of technique, and an excellent memory for its handling. His debt to Ricketts is most evident in the section of his book

Right: This beautiful copy of Rubens' *Isabella Brant* was identified by Sir Sidney Colvin as being by Watteau. The artists also owned another Watteau copy of a Rubens drawing, given to them by Robert Ross.

Below: Ricketts at Kennington Road against a background of art that they admired in their student days.

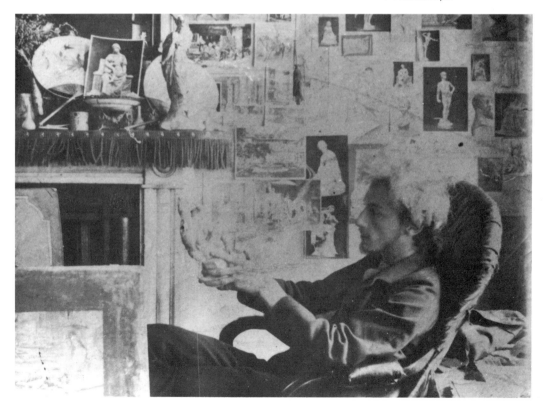

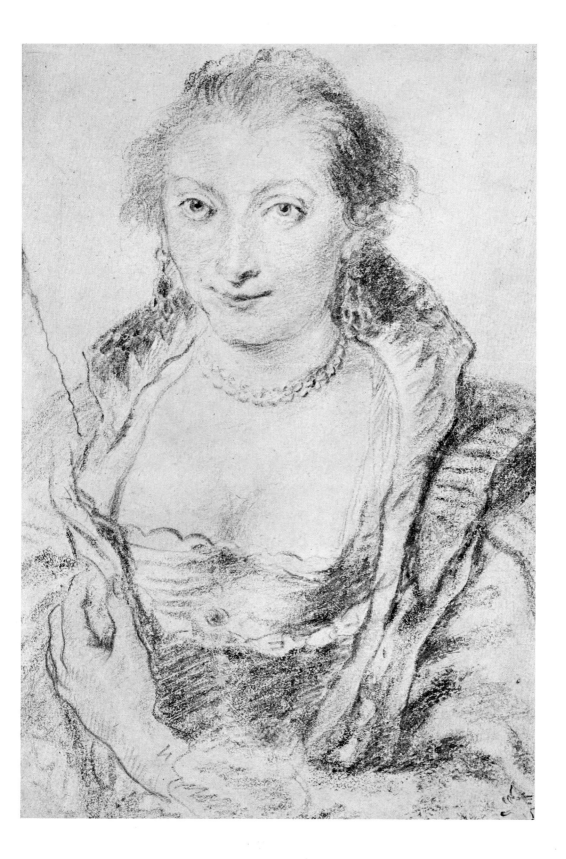

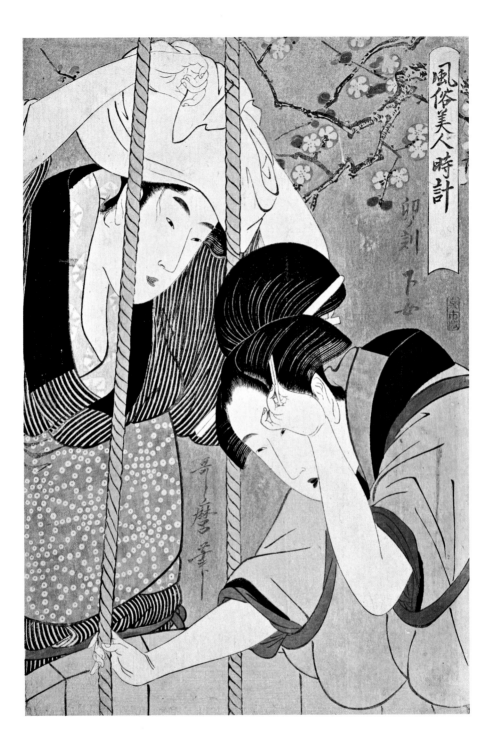

entitled 'Emphasis on Materials'. He discusses several of the artists in whom Ricketts had a particular interest, notably Titian, Puvis de Chavannes and Watts. Holmes's account of the transparent technique employed by Gainsborough and his technical description of the opaque method used by Impressionists are equally enlightening. He condemns attempts by 'Impressionist followers' to paint large pictures (which he considers inappropriate to the technique) 'with the result that no violent forcing of the colour or the design is enough to counterbalance the deadly monotony of raw pigment and uniform spotty handling, displayed on a surface several square feet (or yards) in extent.'

Although Sturge Moore and Holmes responded to painting in their own ways, both freely acknowledged debts to Ricketts. Besides *Armour for Aphrodite*, Sturge Moore wrote monographs on Correggio, Durer and Altdorfer, while Holmes was commissioned by Binyon at the end of the 'nineties to write a short study of Hokusai, before going on (in his days as a museum official) to write about Italian art and the collections of the National Gallery. Ricketts's influence is apparent in the method Sturge Moore adopts in his book about Correggio, while discussing *The Education of Cupid* in the London collection: 'There is evidence of the direct study of some antique torso in the upright figure, and also in the drawing of limbs and extremities – a passage of that flowing refinement that finds its perfect expression in the *Io*, but which is already decided in *Il Giorno*. The Cupid also is no longer half a convention, but wholly

Below: The Drawing Room at Lansdowne House *c*1920.

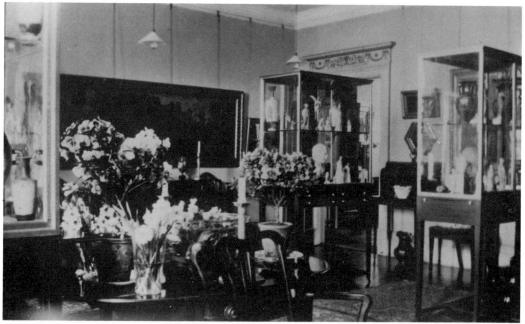

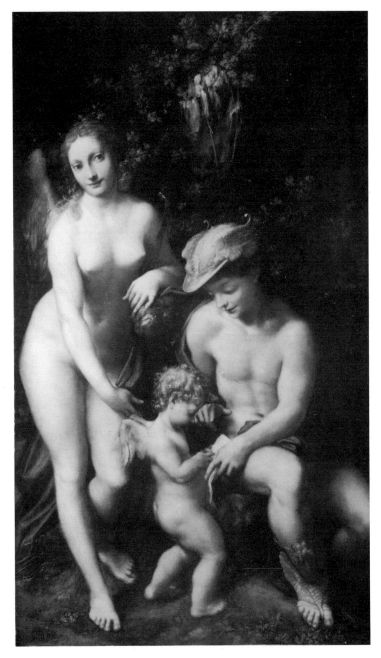

The Education of Cupid by Correggio. Ricketts helped Sturge Moore with a chronology of Correggio's work for his book on that master.

Correggio's invention, with his half-callow wings and their most felicitous articulation with the shoulders, and with that maze of silly curls that covers his head, painted as Vasari well said no other painter ever did or could. The picture has probably been over-cleaned, and so lost its most delicate glazes; perhaps the greenness of the gloom behind disappeared in this way. Signor Ricci imagines the background to have darkened but perhaps, actually painting into a black ground, the watchful master left the picture more as we see it than our ingenious critics, supposing him to pursue a more habitual and less inventive course, imagine.'

Sturge Moore's comments here are based on aesthetic appreciation, backed up by artistic analysis and technical assessment. Unluckily for Ricketts, this type of art criticism was going out of fashion in the years before the First World War, to be replaced by either more popular approaches or more specialised studies. Ricketts viewed his own writing in relation to the great nineteenth-century tradition of such critics as Ruskin or Pater, but the influence of even their opinions on art had waned. Ruskin could be followed only 'with reserve and critical afterthought', as Sir Sidney Colvin warned in his autobiography. Colvin, a Slade Professor at Cambridge, made a much-respected career in the Department of Prints and Drawings at the British Museum. His assessment of Ruskin's work is especially interesting since he had known Ruskin from boyhood. He found in Ruskin's writing ' . . . much misinterpretation of history, a habit of headlong and unquestioning but often quite unwarranted inference from the creations of art to the social conditions lying behind them, with much impassioned misreading of the relations of art in general to nature and to human life: everywhere the fire of genius, everywhere the same lovingly, piercingly intense observation of natural fact: everywhere the same nobleness of purpose and burning zeal for human welfare, the same beautiful felicity and persuasiveness of expression, the same almost unparalleled combination of utter sincerity with infinite rhetorical and dialectical adroitness and resource; but everywhere the same dogmatic and prophetic conviction of being able to set the world right by his own individual insight and judgement on whatever matters might occupy his mind and heart, the same intolerant blindness to all facts and considerations that might tell against his theories, the same liability to intermingle passages of illuminating vision and wisdom with others of petulant, inconsistent, self-contradictory error and misjudgement.' Ricketts, too, reacted against Ruskin. Specifically, he deplored some judgements of taste – Ruskin's feeling for Tintoretto, for example. When Ricketts went to Italy with Shannon in 1899, he wrote 'Tintoretto is perfectly appalling in his vicious contempt for drawing and painting: no man has ever existed in art less equipped as a draughtsman and with a more limited brush-handling, varying between wriggling touches in the flesh and slashing wooden touches in the larger draperies . . . Tintoretto was very properly forgotten, or ranked with Bassano, till Mr Ruskin arrived. Mr Ruskin, who is a lady, was overawed by Tintoretto, just as he might have been silenced by somebody who bawled him down or

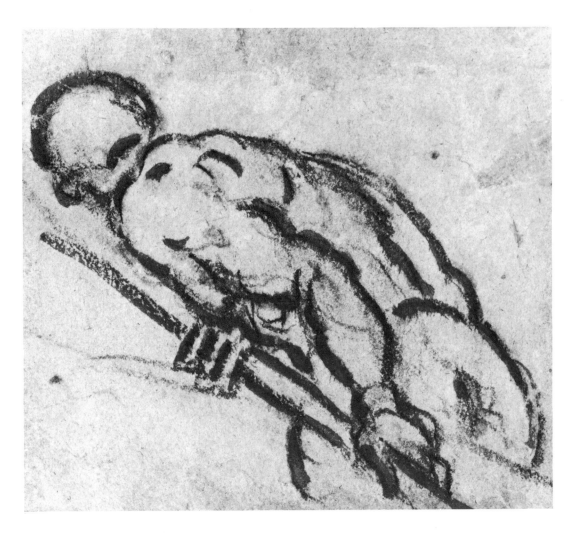

used slang. Reynolds' disregard for Tinto is of a piece with his usual good sense. *Glissons*.'

Ricketts was later to revise this early response to Tintoretto, and the artists were proud of the Tintoretto drawings in their collection, but the reaction from Ruskin was nevertheless strong. The relation between Ricketts's writings on art and Walter Pater's prose seems at first sight closer. As authors, they share the same brilliance of phrase, the blending of personal and artistic judgements, the same high ideals of art. But while Pater could allow himself long passages of psychological speculation, Ricketts felt compelled to discuss more general topics, establishing historical connections and commenting on technical questions. Ricketts might have allowed himself a purple passage in recounting his travels to Egypt and Greece, but in writing about art he was specific.

By the end of the 19th century, art critics were developing a more austere, scientific attitude. In the 1880s Mo-

One of the Tintoretto drawings owned by the artists, this is a study for a figure in *The Battle of Legnano* in the Alte Pinakothek, Munich.

relli had demonstrated in his books how a careful comparison of pictures (especially details) could enable the work of different artists to be identified. This systematic approach was adopted and refined by Bernard Berenson. Heinrich Wölflinn's book on Italian Renaissance art, published in an English edition by 1903, is an example of the historical treatment of styles in art. An exhibition held in London in 1910 was defended by Roger Fry and Clive Bell according to a totally new set of critical principles. Although Ricketts's view of art influenced his friends, and he was widely respected as a connoisseur, his writing on art and artists lost ground to less gifted critics who were more attuned to the preferences of the day. Sturge Moore might attack Berenson in his book on Correggio in a prelude called *Pretensions*; Ricketts might slight Roger Fry by saying in the introduction to *Titian* 'The dates given to the pictures must in most cases be accepted as a symbol of their relation to each other, as I would be the last to imagine that the exact year or month has been revealed to me by some divine inspiration', but the painful fact remained that Fry's writing on Cézanne was a success and Ricketts' book on Titian was not.

What, then, are the qualities of Ricketts's works on art that make them worth re-appraisal? First, enthusiasm; secondly, an admirable style free from jargon; thirdly, a vivid sense of history. These are all the result of a conviction of the importance of art, for Ricketts maintained 'All that survives of a nation is its art', rather as Malraux considered works of art to be footsteps in the sands of time. Further, Ricketts's opinions crystallise an opposition to Impressionism and twentieth-century art movements, for he set out to defend the main European tradition, and the achievement of a great period in art – the nineteenth century. His view, as one formed by both connoisseur and practising artist, is instructive, because it challenges received ideas about modern art and its image.

Looking at European art as a whole, Ricketts pointed out certain moments of dramatic importance, of which the first was when 'The art of Giotto sprang up like a fountain in a desert.' Linking personal lives with artistic development, rather than look for details of derivation in composition or style, Ricketts identified several events that he felt comparable with the emergence of Giotto – the friendship between Brunelleschi, Donatello and Masaccio, or 'When Leonardo returned to Florence and competed with the young Michelangelo, whilst Raphael came and watched them at work.' Characteristically, Ricketts emphasizes the personality of Giorgione. 'He was one of those revolutionists whose influence spreads like a leaven among the chosen few to whom art is an urgent and imperative need. His

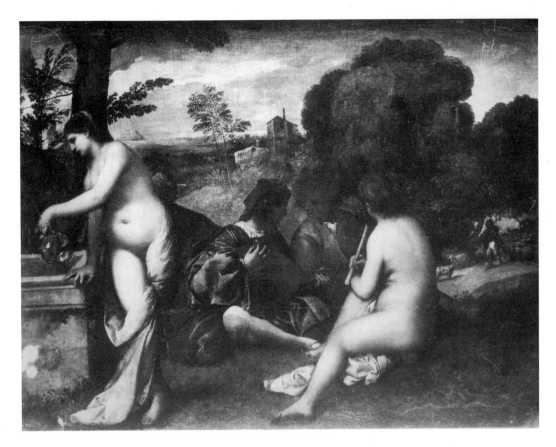

Above: Concert Champêtre by Giorgione. In Giorgione's pictorial formula, 'We note the excursions of a rare fancy, the hold on exquisite realistic incidents, the record of the pleasure of mere eyesight – the flash of light on a tree, a nestling farm or a delicate field-flower.'

example modified the temper and altered the "diction" of Venetian painting as profoundly as the influence of Keats has altered the poetic language and with it the intimate thought of England. We are in the presence of a temperamental force whose immediate action gains significance with time, and against which the powers of "busy commonsense" are of no avail . . . The name of Giorgione stands for a tendency in human thought, his place is among those few who saw in art not the shallow reflection of fact, but who found a means to add to life.'

His view contrasts with the respectful, even reverential, attitude of visitors who travelled to Italy, perhaps with Jacob Burkhardt's *Cicerone*, or a Baedeker guide. Ricketts's taste was strongly personal, and he defended his prejudices with intemperate wit. In 1906 he wrote of his first visit to Siena: 'I do not look forward to my stay there. It is done mainly to annoy my friends, who like to think that because I have not been there I know nothing about Sienese art, when it is a prolonged stay in Siena which really produces that effect.' When he arrived there, his prejudice was confirmed. 'The famous altarpiece of Duccio di Siena ranks with any respectable Russian icon painting in invention and colour. It is a mere piece of furniture. To compare this trash to Giotto is a profanation so singular that one understands people admiring Cézanne or Gauguin. Siena belongs to the wrong side of Italy and to bogus Italian lovers, that is as far as the art is concerned, the place is delightful. Sodoma is insignificant and on the whole fraudulent, a survival from the time of Ruskin when people said they liked what bored them profoundly.'

If Ricketts disliked something, he did not stop to be bored. After visiting an exhibition with Legros, he recorded in amazement that Legros, having just seen masterpieces by Velasquez, then insisted 'on going round to the modern work and sneering and sniffing in front of worthless pictures by worthless Spaniards. Even the artist,' he commented, 'is tainted by the democratic notion of competition and comparison. With me, art is a function like eating. I choose the dishes I like best; it never occurs to me to taste dishes I dislike, that I may say funny things about them.'

One of Ricketts's touchstones was the work of Titian, an artist about whom he had the opportunity to write in his book on the Prado, and also his chosen subject for a full-scale study. Ricketts was satisfied with his book, re-reading it in 1914 'with something like astonishment at its shrewdness, sanity and insight. . . What struck me most was the compact thinking, the substance which a critic would have worked out into the *leit-motif* of an article used in a sentence.' His book was in direct competition with two others, one by a German art historian Gronau, and another by a professional writer on the arts, Claude Phillips. It is better than either, especially in the evocation of places and periods. It is also less mundane than the first and more specific than the second. Titian was a heroic figure for Ricketts, both as 'the father of modern painting', and as a man whose own prestige raised the standing of other artists in his time. Furthermore, Titian, with Giorgione, represented a type of painting which Ricketts and Shannon in their own way sought to re-create. 'We first found in Venice what the Renaissance called "poesies" and idylls; that is, pictures of an allusive and poetic bent in which we detect a love of beauty for its own sake and an *a priori* wish to charm and fascinate.' Ricketts's words here recall the terms in which he praised Shannon's work.

In the context of his assessment of Giorgione, Ricketts regards Titian's early career as subordinate to Giorgione's in invention. As he did not search for meanings in paintings, Ricketts felt that *Sacred and Profane Love* marked Titian's passage out of 'his early abrupt mood' and demonstrated 'all that can be said in his lyrical mood'. He records an iconographical interpretation of the subject as Medea listening to the persecution of Venus, who urges her to love Jason, but goes on to argue that the artistic

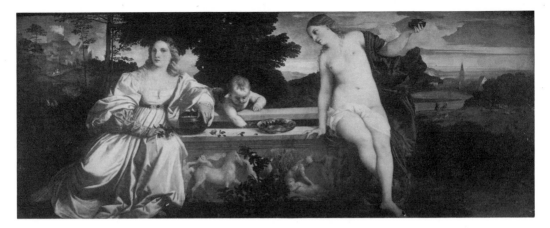

qualities of this work make it 'One of the world's loveliest pictures. In no other work of art, *Annunciation* or *Visitation* shall we discover two figures so enchantingly related to each other; in no other design is the eye more charmed by perfect spacing and ordering of the composing element. Few figures in art possess to the same degree this profound and feminine graciousness which characterises the self-absorbed figure of Medea, as yet unconscious of a tragic destiny; no figure invented by Titian or any other master surpasses in beauty of line the sinuous and enchanting curves which express the contour of the Venus; the invention of the crimson cloak which buttresses the figure, the extended arm against the sky, are each supreme inventions in design.'

Titian's next phase, in which he achieved maturity, represented the balanced art which Ricketts most admired. He describes the *Assunta* as a model for religious art, transcending style. Ricketts and Shannon had been impressed by the painting from the first time they saw it, and Ricketts wrote to Holmes in 1899, 'The *Assunta* knocked us flat with admiration.' Titian's last works, on the other hand, lacked the poise that Ricketts admired. He sees the portraits as highly charged with emotion, but 'less himself.' He therefore received the *Pieta* more coolly than Titian's earlier mature works. Ricketts's values and the nature of his criticism are clearly seen in his conclusion of *Titian* – as Sturge Moore remarked, when Ricketts praised, he praised indeed:

'What is there more to say which can add anything of value which we shall not find better expressed in the master's paintings? Beauty of fact, beauty of invention, beauty in the method of interpretation, each is present in his pictures, wealth and power and order, the expression of each is constant in his art. We may hint at something essential in his art when we allow – that like the culture of the Latin races it is sane, central and sensuous. I might gain a ready agreement with me were I to say that Titian is the most typical figure of the Renaissance, and that his paintings best express its aim, but that movement was too complex to be contained even in the range of the master;

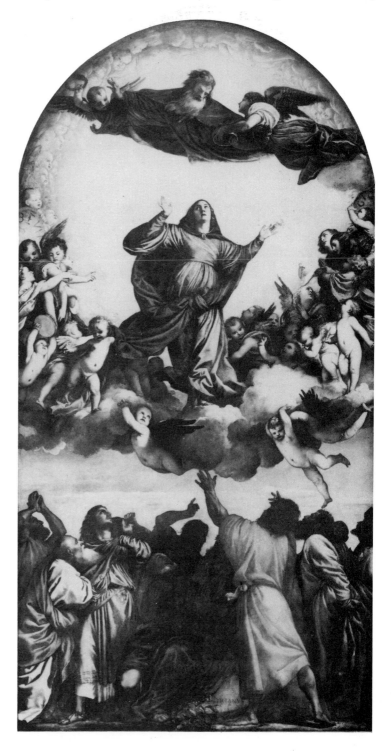

L'Assunta by Titian. In 'The best-known and most popular of Titian's masterpieces ... the face of Mary satisfies us as expressing ecstasy in a human type.' We enjoy 'the garland of children who surround her', and there is 'the rich simplicity of the group of gigantic apostles who crowd the stage below with a few grand gestures.'

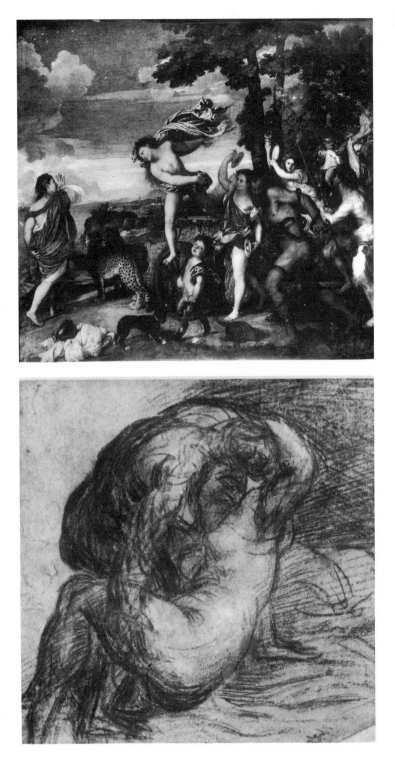

Bacchus and Ariadne by Titian, 1523. 'We see no haste, nothing but the most consummate and tender practices: the flesh is softened in its glazes by those touches of the fingers with which Titian is said by Palma Giovane to have painted at the end. Look at the melting eyes of the little fauns softened by the touch of the master's finger – it is the very essence of a great tradition or practice.'

One of the most remarkable finds made for the collection, the perceptive attribution to Titian remains unchallenged. Ricketts gave the drawing *Jupiter and Io* as a title, but the subject is not certain.

he does not typify it in its entirety, his genius remains more local, more Italian. There are ardour, richness, ease – all the gifts of the sun in his work; in temper he is the most

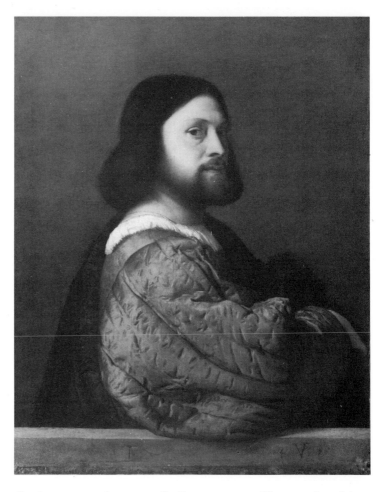

Latin among the great Italian masters. He translated into the terms of painting something characteristic of the race to whom we owe the pattern of civility and the grammar of our arts. If the frescoes of Raphael express a profound harmony of character and the range and richness of the culture of the Renaissance, Titian's paintings reflect the vitality of the race to whom that culture was acceptable. Greatness in art has been defined as 'strength tempered by sweetness' and if we recognise in the unrivalled art of Michelangelo (to whom this definition has been applied) a superhuman strength, tempered by a sense of something beyond power, and by a sense of compassion equal to his strength, with Titian there is no such contrast in aim, we leave the abrupt mountain world of thought for happier tablelands spreading out beneath the light under which it is good to live; his art is as rich as Italy, profound and tranquil as the Mediterranean, his power has its roots in the realm of a nature outwardly placid, yet varied and strong with the strength of perfect sanity and health ripened by the richness of the sun.'

95

Artistic Tempers

'One quality', wrote Ricketts, 'counts for most, namely the essential quality of the artistic temper of the painter. It is the player himself who counts, not the rules of the game he chances to play.' Having considered such artists as Titian and Giorgione, Ricketts extended his critical analysis, introducing Rubens by way of comparison:

'I have described the art of Titian as illustrating "the truth of outward things"; we might say that Rubens illustrated "the effectiveness of outward things". Life, beauty and passion is found in him – not that power of concentration we admire in the great art of Titian – but a generous welcome and a large power of affirmation.' He wrote of Rubens's 'sense of beauty which is more joyous than intimate', and noted that he 'deals nobly and generously with the broad facts of life and history, its variety and movement . . . His men and women are broadly drawn in character in the essentials of their respective sex; he renders perfectly the force, beauty and emphasis of animal life, the force and effectiveness of all power and emotions.'

Given Ricketts's desire for harmony in art, it is understandable that he had reservations about art that was dominated by emotional force. This is clear in his writing on El Greco, whom he compares with Tintoretto:

'The aim of Tintoretto was sensational, but eloquent in its sensationalism; its tendency was declamatory and romantic, tending towards an emphatic statement of dramatic or romantic effects. With El Greco the imaginative impulse thickens and twists upon itself; there is even less balance than in the Italian; there is even less room, even less breathing-space for sequence of thought, or for constructive vision; he gives you a sort of shorthand of Tintoretto, and later on mere jottings and hints at a method of his own; at times his figures have the lithe and trenchant aspect of a sword.' Furthermore, 'No one would apply to El Greco the statement that art is the expression of that which the artist likes best in life; his choice would seem to be governed by another craving, and to have been of the nature that makes

96

a man lean over a precipice to see if he will feel faint or dizzy, or a patient touch a wound to see if it will hurt.'

The painting of Velasquez was more to Ricketts's liking. (Shannon's professional experience as a portrait painter certainly added vitality to discussions between the artists on this subject, as in many others.) Although he felt that Velasquez's reputation was too high in France and England, Ricketts acknowledged the persuasion of 'the freshness and delicacy of his vision, the grave and subtle charm of his personality.' He went on to relate Velasquez's painting to the work of other artists: 'His effort expresses neither the joy and the ample resources of life itself, as with Rubens; nor its tragedy and comedy, as with Rembrandt; nor its spiritual aspirations, as with Michael Angelo; he barely goes beyond what might be brought into a cool grey room; he has shown the delicacy, the nobility even, that lies in common things – the beauty of shadows, the transfiguring

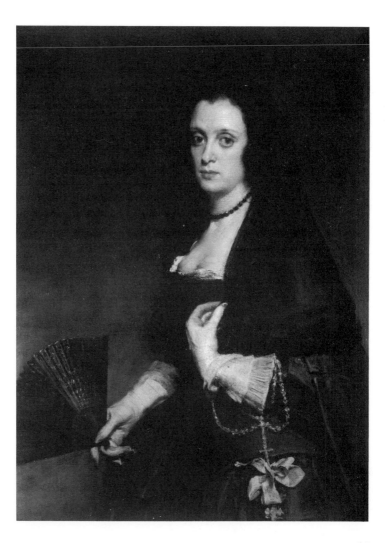

The Lady with the Fan by Velasquez. 'As a painter of women he has produced two masterpieces, *The Lady in Blue* in Berlin, *The Lady with the Fan* in London ... Neither expressing the noblest temperaments only, nor delineating in the human face only the stronger and baser passions of the human soul, he finds a middle course full of delicate gravity.'

charm of a ray of light. By the carriage of a head, the poise of a hand, he startles us into delighted attention. He painted every-day people – tranquil, well-bred people. We do not feel, as with Rembrandt, that they are poised at some climax of their lives or thought; or, as with Titian, that his sitters are princes in very deed, in thought, or by the trace on them of things suffered and done.' But then, 'Velasquez was less lucky than Titian in the humanity he had to paint; that Titian had for sitters Charles V and Aretino, while Velasquez only painted the phlegmatic *viveur* Philip IV and the charlatan Olivaren.' Comparing Velasquez with Holbein, Ricketts continued, 'Holbein's aim seems literal enough, yet his grip upon character is more tenacious; nowhere in the work of Velasquez can we watch the current of delicate thought which we note in some masterpieces of Holbein – the *Erasmus* for instance.' And Velasquez's 'delicate gravity' is what makes him 'the supreme painter of children. The still half-flower-like texture of their skin and hair, their flower-like eyes, their gravity when left to themselves – all this has been caught and rendered in a way that no other artist has been able to rival. We have nothing to do with the mother's darling type, but we have an extraordinary insight into the tremulous consciousness of early childhood. Compared with Velasquez's portraits of children the famous children of Reynolds are too arch, too blooming; the children of Gainsborough too sentimental and appealing.'

Below: Watteau's *Les Charmes de la Vie*. We see here Watteau as 'the painter-poet of leisure, the lover of heartsease, of peace and tranquility where contentment counts for most. His is the pastoral mood which loves to dwell in the sun and listen to the ripening hours counted by the pulses of a brook.'

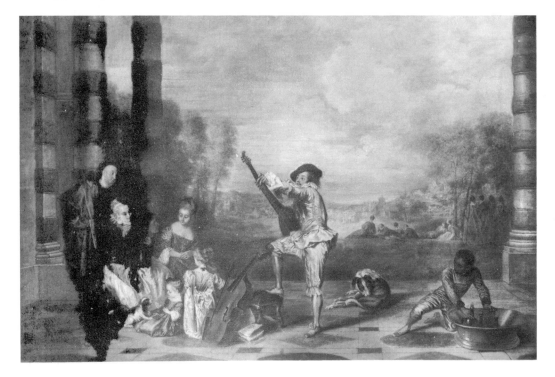

Ricketts was also charmed by Watteau's sense of grace – a characteristic that had also attracted the Goncourt brothers, Verlaine, and Beardsley – and well expressed its nature in *Pages on Art*: 'To the lover of contemplation, to the man who would nurse his mood and toy with his melancholy, Watteau has brought his pictures which are devoted to the expression of an enchanted isolation and repose: his is the power to conjure us away to places beyond our time or his, where we can saunter in idyllic woods and in the delicate gardens of old palaces of art where reality has become entranced.' Ricketts was aware of the haunting quality in Watteau's work described in a Michael Field poem about a Watteau painting in the Dresden gallery.

On the autumnal grass the pairs
Of lovers couch themselves and raise
A facile merriment that dares
Surprise the vagueness of the sun
October to a veil has spun
About the heads and forest-ways
      Delicious light
Of gold so pure it half-refines to white.

Yet Venus from this world of love,
Of haze and warmth has turned; as yet
None feels it save the trees above
The roses in their soft decline
And one ill-humoured libertine.
Soon shall all hearts forget
      The vows they swore
And the leaves strew the glade's untrodden floor.

It was to be expected that Ricketts and Shannon would respond to charm in art. Ricketts's article on Charles Conder describes the artist's qualities as 'delightful in colour, design, and in the sense of wit and romance which they evoke, the sense of luxury which they express and the love for beautiful things that pass away, like laughter and music, the mirage of noon, the magic of the night, the perfume of flowers, and youth, and life.' His immediate response to charm, however, failed to make Ricketts lose sight of major developments in European art. Titian's true pupils, he felt, were other masters, Rubens, Velasquez, Van Dyck and Reynolds, while Watteau's art was influenced by both Rubens and Venetian pastorals. As for nineteenth-century art, Ricketts valued it highly, though he did not consider landscapes as the main product of the period. Romanticism was the living spirit of the century, whether in England or France. In a passage on Fantin-Latour, he argued that the romantic spirit had breathed more life into individual artists' works than could be found in Impressionism.

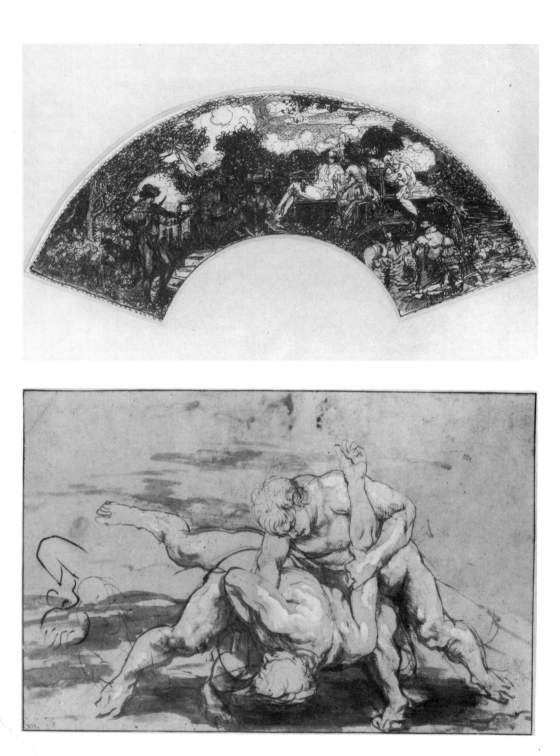

'By the unexpected death of Fantin-Latour,' Ricketts commented, 'France is deprived of one of her most exclusive and individual artists, and a link is broken that connects the present with the art movement in France which was first hailed by Baudelaire, and was destined to develop

A drawing based on an antique marble group, *Two Wrestlers* in the Uffizi, Florence, dramatised by Rubens, 'one of the world's two supreme draughtsmen.'

100

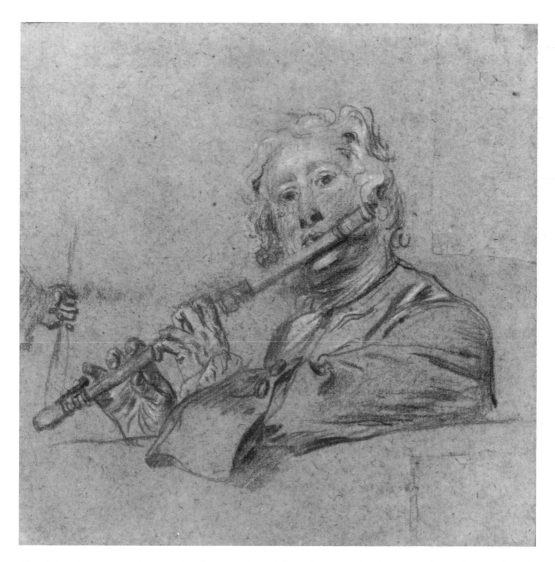

Man playing a Flute, a charming drawing by Watteau, bought in 1903, with which Ricketts was especially pleased.

Above left:
Design for a fan by Charles Conder. Ricketts predicted of Conder 'his fans will some day become classics ... One of his fans does well enough in a frame; its true value becomes manifest when it is mounted and so becomes a living ornament or accessory of dress revealing in its countless harmonies of colour and inventions of detail much which might well be studied by some couturier of the future.'

in the one hand into impressionism, on the other to break up into isolated personalities which were opposed to it and its catchwords "values", "division of tone", "open air", and other casual and isolated subjects of enquiry. Among those "personal" painters who have stood outside the pale of impressionism Degas and Whistler stand midway, Puvis de Chavannes stands beyond, Legros is in opposition, while Fantin stands apart.'

Fantin-Latour's lithographs are singled out for praise: 'A superb series of lithographs, done ostensibly under the inspiration of the great romantic musicians, but which in their heroines – *Astarte*, *Dido* or *Kundry* – appear as the sisters of the *Io* or *Antiope* of Correggio. Something which lingers in the art of Prudhon and Corot glimmers in these designs for the last time: they are the elegy or swan-song of romanticism.'

Ricketts was a fervent admirer of Puvis de Chavannes, from whom he and Shannon had sought advice as students. Later in life, Ricketts bought a drawing and recorded in his diary, 'Great red-letter day. One of Puvis de Chavannes's nine stupendous sanguines for the Amiens Museum decorations was bought by me at E. J. van Wisselingh's for the huge sum of one hundred and thirty-four pounds. I burst into perspiration at the sight of it, so great was my lust of possession. It had just been refused by the British Museum owing to size and cost: the latter, from their point of view, is a good excuse, since they do not know how important Puvis is, and how rare is a drawing of this order.'

The importance of Puvis de Chavannes was quite clear to Ricketts. He wrote of the artist's '. . . new spirit pervad-

A study for *Le Travail* by Puvis de Chavannes for the murals at Amiens. Ricketts found in Puvis' work 'a preoccupation with the finding of a kind of drawing which would express the major saliencies and characteristics and yet form part of the design of the whole picture.'

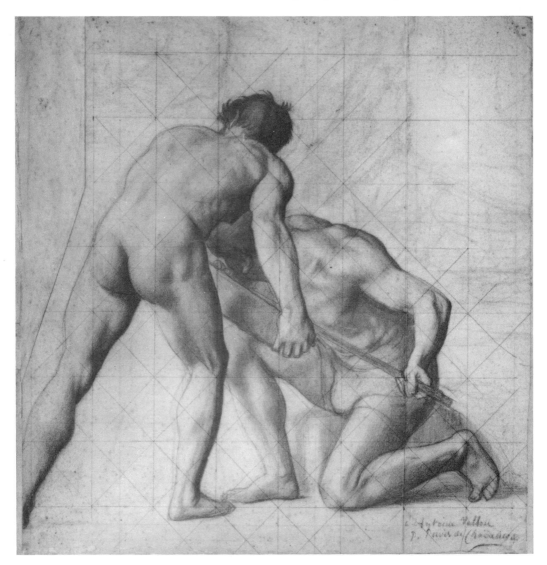

ing even his earliest works, which is not Roman as with Poussin, not neo-Greek as with Ingres, nor Ionian and exotic as with Chasseriau. To the efforts of these great artists towards a plastic and poetic synthesis Puvis de Chavannes has added a more racy sense of the French soil, a more human and comprehensive vision, and in the construction, method and aspect of his paintings he has brought a mass of new qualities which rank him among the great designers in the history of art.' The sense in which Puvis achieved a 'poetic and elastic synthesis' is made more explicit: 'Puvis de Chavannes has rendered the countless moods belonging to the seasons over land and sea, in the dawn, noon and twilight . . . these effects form part in a noble scheme in which man has not been banished out of nature (to be replaced by the temper of the artist), but in which he figures in the eternally engrossing drama of work and repose, effort of thought, under the spell of passion, tenderness and meditation: in movements of effort and moods of compassion . . . like all great masters, besides the moods in which his art is stimulating as a tonic, and beyond the possibilities of the common man, Puvis de Chavannes paints also those moods of ecstasy in which we find the love of beauty and ease and grace which have also their power of consolation.'

The synthesis that Ricketts admired as the achievement of Puvis also attracted him in the work of Watts, whom Ricketts describes in his review of the Watts exhibition at the Royal Academy: 'A great technician, a master painter, a pioneer and experimentalist in his craft: he is in this matter the great event since Turner, and the most dignified painter since Reynolds.' Quoting Fromentin's remark that the art of painting is to express the invisible by the visible, Ricketts writes, 'The invisible! The pulsations in the air about a spiritual manifestation, the peculiar rhythm belonging to "*Les gestes insolites*", the appeal to our emotions by some intuitive use of line, mass, tone, and colour, or expression – this poetic, or emotional gift has been at the command of this master in many of his imaginative designs. There is the unexpressed image left on the brain between the painted gesture and the one which preceded it or must follow it. Botticelli has this gift, Tintoretto often fails in this and remains declamatory: in this Delacroix rarely fails.' Ricketts's review mainly concerns technique. He prefers to leave the poetic quality of the works to be at least partly remembered by his readers in the words of Swinburne writing on *The Life of Pygmalion* – a helpful reminder of the company Ricketts keeps in his prose: Swinburne, as well as Pater and Wilde.

Fantin-Latour represented technical mastery of a medium, Puvis de Chavannes a monumental quality, and

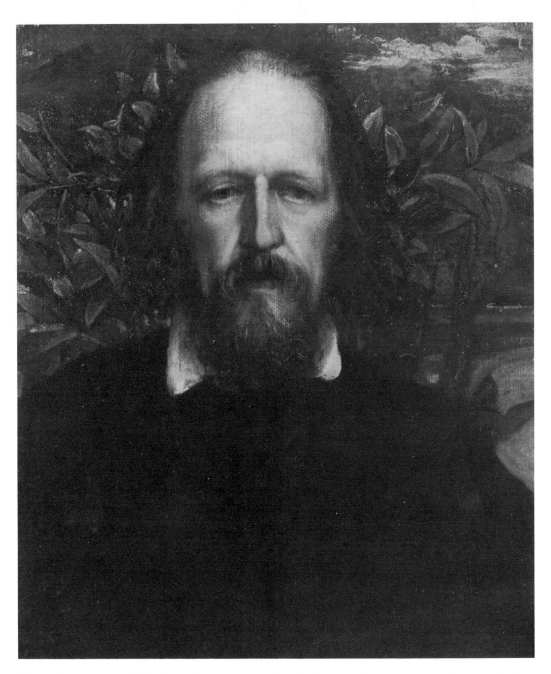

Watts harmony. Added to these successes of nineteenth-century art, Ricketts saw inspired qualities in Blake, Rossetti and Burne-Jones. Not only did Ricketts and Shannon admire these artists they also acquired examples of their work. They owned oil sketches and drawings by Delacroix, whose views on art and society Ricketts much respected. In dismissing the idea that landscape painting was the main triumph of the century, Ricketts quoted an opinion expressed by Delacroix, that it was 'the minor art of a

Alfred, Lord Tennyson by G. F. Watts. Ricketts shared a general admiration for Watts' noted portraits of men, but he gave special praise to his mastery of technique.

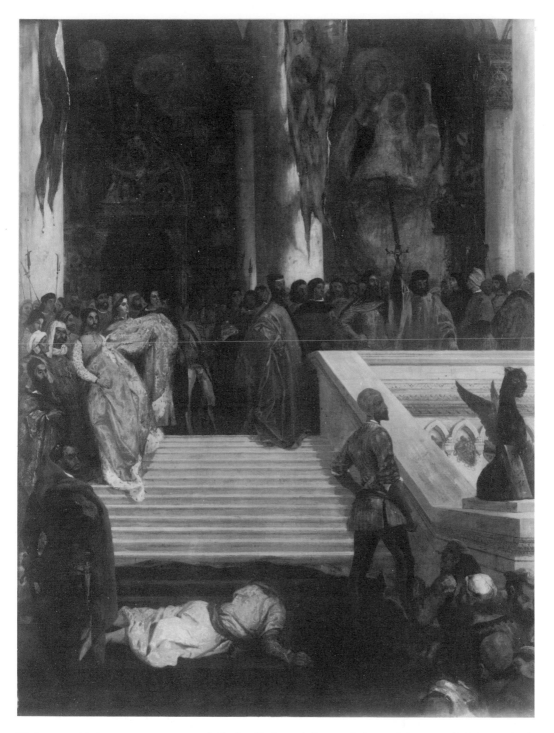

The Execution of the Doge, Marino Faliero by Delacroix. 'The vistas opened up to the world by the great musicians have their counterpart in the poetic painters of the century'

specialist'. Delacroix's social position and his artistic achievements were even more significant for Ricketts in his assessment of the artist's role in society. He saw the nineteenth century as a period when the world had 'No palaces for its great painters to decorate, no deeds it cared to

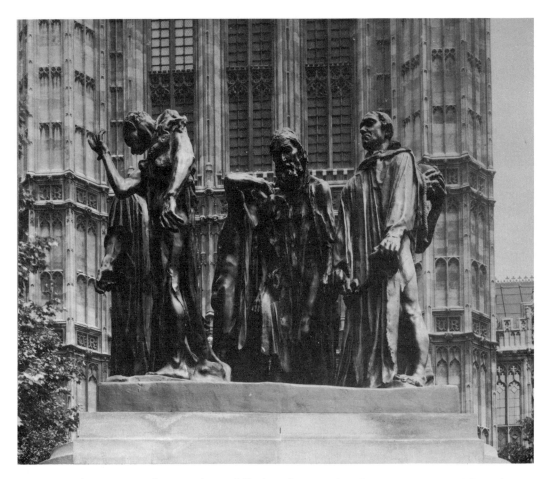

entrust to its great sculptors; the public has favoured only the men who resembled it, and bidden the artist to make bricks without straw.'

Delacroix was for Ricketts, as he was for Baudelaire, the epitome of Romanticism. In 1901 Ricketts delighted in reading Baudelaire's critical views of the Salon to find the mention of a latent imaginative quality, in Delacroix that was 'Not dramatic merely, but "musical"; by that I do not mean the melodious, the harmonious, the rhythmic element, but something more.' This flicker of thought is typical of Ricketts, who liked to find analogies in different arts.

It also separated Ricketts from critics who looked at art in a more technical way, or sought to create an aesthetic theory of painting. The morphological approach of Morelli and the aesthetic theories of 'tactile values' from Berenson, 'pneumatic values' from Vernon Lee, or 'significant form' from Clive Bell – these are cases in point. Ricketts's writing describes sensuous responses to works of art, but in doing so uses almost conversational words like 'discursive', or 'delightful', and occasionally ventures a metaphor like this one on the end of the eighteenth century: 'The music of

The Burghers of Calais by Auguste Rodin. 'The greatest of living artists' was President of the International Society, and commanded such respect that this sculpture was bought by subscription and placed outside the Houses of Parliament.

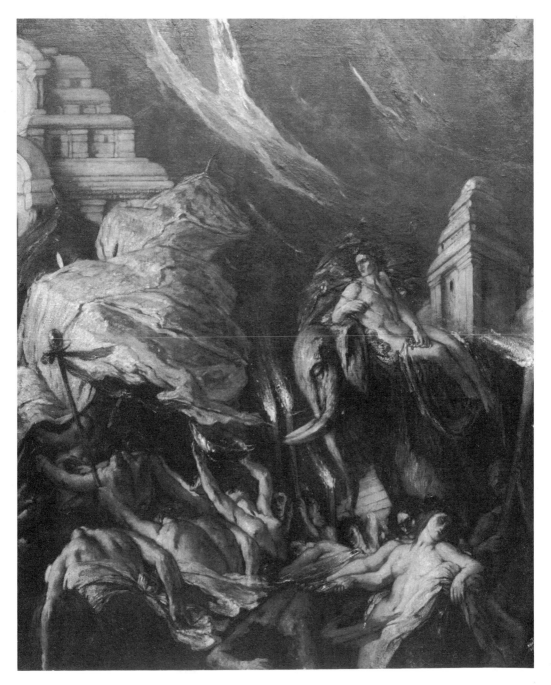

Bacchus in India by Ricketts. Ricketts was pleased when he found a critic who 'discovered the influence of Delacroix and Moreau on my work as a compliment, whilst Holmes in his British way viewed it as a score against me and looked to see me blush.'

Gluck and Mozart became lost for a while in the sound of the hungry tramp of the Revolution.'

Ricketts may not pretend to a philosophy of art but there is no doubt where he stands. He is an idealist, conscious of a 'fruitful feud between realism under many disguises and idealism under many names, or to put it briefly, the struggle between observation put into immediate terms of painting and experience translated into terms of art.'

Collecting

The skill of Ricketts and Shannon as connoisseurs and collectors is apparent in their bequest to the Fitzwilliam Museum, Cambridge, one of its most important gifts. The treasures in their collection ranged from Egyptian antiquities, Greek vases and classical gems to outstanding drawings by old masters including Rembrandt, Rubens and Watteau, and nineteenth-century works by Delacroix, Millet, Puvis de Chavannes and the English painters, Millais, Alfred Stevens, Rossetti and Burne-Jones. Most of their fine collection of Japanese prints passed to the British Museum.

Having decided to leave their main collection to the Fitzwilliam Museum (after a visit by Shannon to Cambridge), the artists as joint owners each made wills in the other's favour and, although the bequest is registered by both the Fitzwilliam and British museums under the name of Shannon, who outlived Ricketts by six years, it is good to see that items on display are correctly acknowledged as part of the Ricketts and Shannon collection. The collector's mark used by the artists on a number of drawings and prints is recorded in the catalogue of such marks compiled by Fritz Lugt.

It is difficult to discover which of the artists was responsible for a particular acquisition. We know that Ricketts made some of the spectacular finds, such as the small circular panel which was for a time believed to have been part of the frame of an altarpiece by Masaccio. Ricketts seems to have been more easily tempted than Shannon to buy in new fields – a letter discussing prices in the 'twenties comments on bargains to be found in ceramics, but notes that Shannon was inclined to concentrate their search on more drawings. Some major purchases were the decision of Shannon, who was very interested in Japanese art. Sale catalogues give either Ricketts or Shannon as the purchaser, but this cannot be taken without corroboration as evidence of an individual decision to buy, as acquisitions seem almost always to have been thoroughly discussed between the two friends.

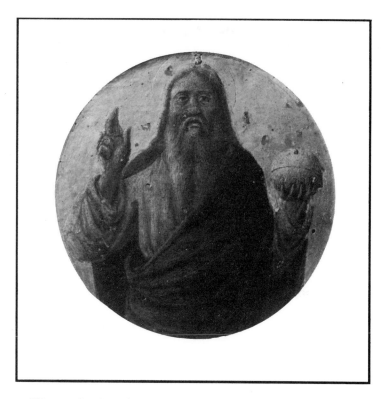

This small roundel from a Renaissance frame was once thought to be by Masaccio, from his Naples alterpiece. Ricketts wrote in 1908 'I bought it for thirty-five bob as a Russian icon.' Ricketts and Shannon gave it to the National Gallery, London, where it is now relegated to the early Florentine school.

The artists' attitude to money and the value of their collection was straightforward – they bought with the greatest care, believing rightly that their taste was justified and the value of their collection would reflect their discernment. The unsuccessful purchase of shares with a windfall left to Shannon encouraged them to restrict their investment to art, but they did not speculate in art for which they had no feeling. As a result, some of their acquisitions increased substantially in value, whereas others remained of considerable interest but little financial worth. At the time of their deaths, the large collection of Burne-Jones drawings, for example, was assessable at a low price, while other items, especially old master drawings, had appreciated dramatically in value. Bottomley recorded that in the last year of his life Ricketts said 'I was lately offered £27,000 for the old-master drawings in the dining room: I am not sure how I ought to describe the sensation . . . I believe I was awe struck [as] when £1000 were offered for the Rembrandt alone, and I remembered we gave 15s. for it when we were young and beginners.' The collection was an investment upon which the artists could draw if the need arose. On moving to their home in Albert Road, they sold a painting by Puvis de Chavannes, and further sales were needed to pay for the care of Shannon in his illness.

The loss of items from the collection through sale, as gifts, or in the disposal of books, furniture and effects after

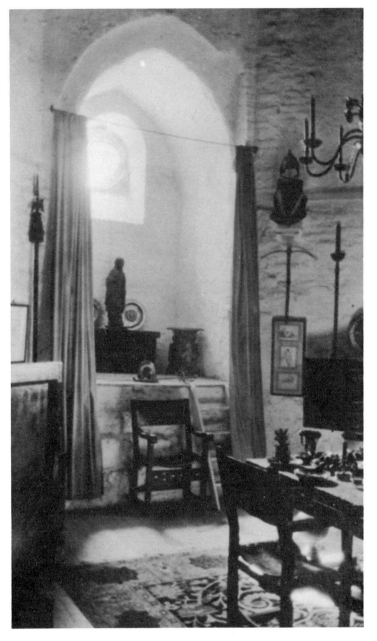

Shannon's death, hinder attempts to identify those that
formed a part of it at any given time. It is frustrating to
know that Ricketts and Shannon owned a painting by
Daumier without being able to determine which painting.
Even so, the collection as we know it demonstrates their
taste in a thousand works of art in public collections.

In their various homes, Ricketts and Shannon allowed
their collection to have a presence of its own. While they
acquired objects suitable for their settings – armour and
old oak for Chilham Castle, and eighteenth-century furni-

A view of Lansdowne House showing the fragment of the torso of Apollo illustrated on p.120 *in situ*.

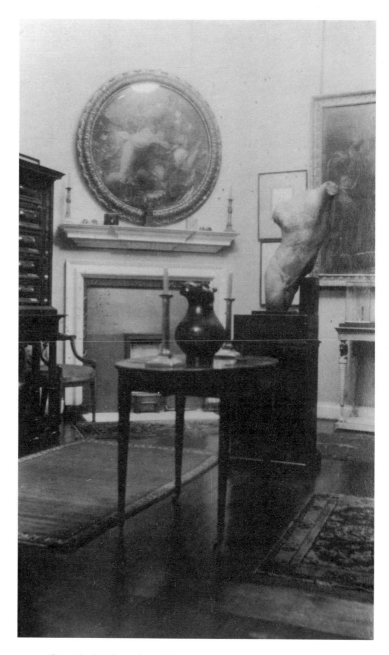

ture for their London homes – they did not allow the background to dominate the objects. So much is clear from Cecil Lewis's description of Ricketts's studio: 'He had no sense of comfort. The easy chair with its deep feather cushions into which you "relax" was anathema to him. His "easy" chairs cost 35s. and were almost devoid of padding; his sofa was as uncomfortable as a waiting room seat at a railway station. All were covered with blue cotton cloth at a shilling a yard . . . His ash-trays were saucers, his palette an old plate, his warmth a square black-leaded stove.'

Ricketts said he lived like a grandee, in simple personal style, but officially in state; and that state was the splendour of the salon, with its Egyptian antiquities, Greek vases and Tanagra statuettes. Cecil Lewis has left a vivid description of the dining room:

'The dining room, the bridge from work to entertainment, was the most perfect I have ever seen. Ricketts had that unique quality of taste which enabled him to distinguish an object of merit whatever its period or use. You would not think that old master drawings would be at home with a Chinese bird-cage; you would not think that red and green marble-topped tables could live in amity; you would fancy that Empire chairs might swear at Morris chintzes, French knives could not harmonise with Georgian silver, and a modern blue glass bowl could never stand at the foot of a Grecian statuette; the whole could certainly not be lit hard with clear bulbs hanging from sixpenny porcelain shades. Yet, strangely, all combined to give a sense of luxury and elegance that was incomparable. Each object, being in itself perfect, added its lustre to the whole, so that the room, which was, winter and summer, filled with flowers, glowed with a radiant and compelling beauty.'

This description of the collection as it was in the later part of the 'twenties shows just how far the passion for collecting had taken the two artists from their pinned-up photographs of student days in Lambeth. There is no doubt that they were well placed to make such a collection in London at that time. The sale rooms were very active. Holmes, who used to bid on behalf of the artists from time to time in the Vale Press days, noted that the dealers and collectors knew each other well, and watched the sale rooms very carefully. This competitive circle provided a valuable education, and Ricketts and Shannon made good use of their opportunities. Their interest in pictures was partly technical, a search for material that would be of use or reference in their own artistic work, but for drawings there was no such limitation. It was to their advantage as collectors that they had almost no interest in landscapes, which took a considerable portion of the market in English art out of their province. Also they did not specialise, buying for quality in whatever period, civilisation or medium opportunity offered. A friend's description of Ricketts as a collector of genius gains further interest from a comment, in another context, by Ricketts: 'Success or perfect good luck are integral elements in the composition of all genius; the work is of the spirit, and knows no place.' The nature of the artists' particular achievement becomes clearer in comparison with other collectors and connoisseurs. In a period when historical knowledge about works of art was

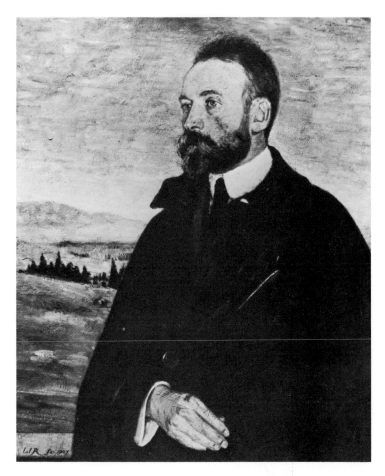

Bernard Berenson by William Rothenstein. A portrait in a Renaissance vein painted in 1907.

increasing rapidly, Ricketts did not undertake a systematic study of paintings and their provenance. Several of his contemporaries made carefully planned collections of photographs; in doing so, Berenson became one of the leading scholars of Italian Renaissance painting, Sir Robert Witt founded the reference library of photographs of paintings that is named after him, and Lord Conway created a similar photographic archive of architecture and sculpture, now the Conway Library. Ricketts's attitude was closer to that of Herbert Horne, who asserted that he could buy drawings with the money he saved by not collecting photographs.

The growth of the art market from the 1890s gave rise to a new class of scholar, whose main occupation lay in advising dealers and rich collectors. Berenson collected pictures on behalf of Mrs Isabella Stewart Gardner of Boston and, more significantly, advised Lord Duveen, the most successful of all dealers of the period. Berenson's field of expertise was therefore at the highest level of the art market. Sir Hugh Lane, a picturesque figure of the period, made considerable money as a dealer and formed the idea

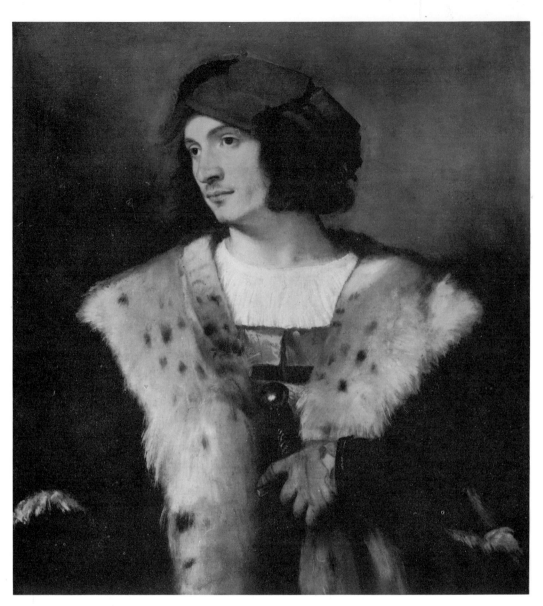

of making Dublin an important gallery. Although he was especially interested in Impressionism, his finds as a connoisseur include a fine portrait by Titian, which had gone unrecognised by Christie's, but is now one of the treasures of the Frick collection in New York. Roger Fry, who worked for the Metropolitan Museum in New York, was among scholars who won official posts as advisers to collectors, again in positions that called for judgements about some of the most expensive pictures on the market.

A further source of income for scholars was through the provision of certificates of attribution, stating the view of the scholar that a painting was by a particular artist. The magazine *Apollo* edited by Tancred Borenius was one which

Titian's *Portrait of a Man in a Red Cap*. 'In a darkened and dirty condition' at Christie's, Ricketts 'imagined this beautiful Giorgionesque work to be an early work of Francesco Vecellio.' After cleaning, 'the brown background had become a harmonious warm grey, the glove and fur which I had thought indifferent, revealed the tender pigment of the master; the painting of the linen *pâte sur pâte* was a practice of Titian. The work stood out..a masterpiece.' The shrewd purchaser was Sir Hugh Lane, not Ricketts.

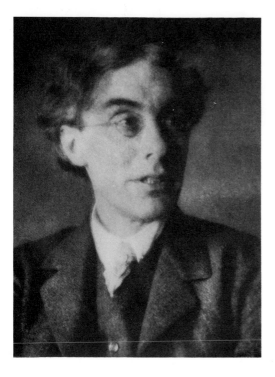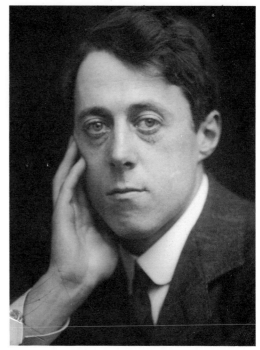

discussed the authenticity of works. Ricketts refused to
write for it, considering that it advanced Borenius's personal interests. Eventually Ricketts accepted a post as adviser to the National Gallery of Canada, but in that job he
was not advising purchase at the highest prices – more
important pictures were bought, often on his advice, by Sir
Edmund Davis.

The state of the art market contributed to the success
achieved by Ricketts and Shannon as collectors. Many of
the best-informed connoisseurs were concerned professionally with painting, and the detailed study of drawings in
the context of art history was still a thing of the future.
Further, the two artists' friends included individuals without any financial interest in the art market, with whom
opinions could be exchanged. Ricketts's letters and diaries
make this plain; he was on excellent terms with Laurence
Binyon in the British Museum, discussed forgeries and
Tanagra figures with Cecil Smith in the same museum and
made recommendations and assisted in the attribution of
Greek vases for Sir Sydney Cockerell at the Fitzwilliam.
He was also consulted by the young Beazley – then at the
beginning of an outstanding career as a student of Greek
vase painting – besides serving on the committee of the
National Art Collections Fund. The artists' single-minded
aim to collect works of quality from the less expensive areas
of the art market and their personal reputation as connoisseurs were two main factors in their success.

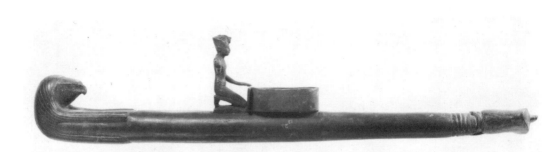

Above: An exceptional example
of a type of royal censer
inscribed with the name of King
Amaris (570-526 BC) in
hollow-cast bronze.

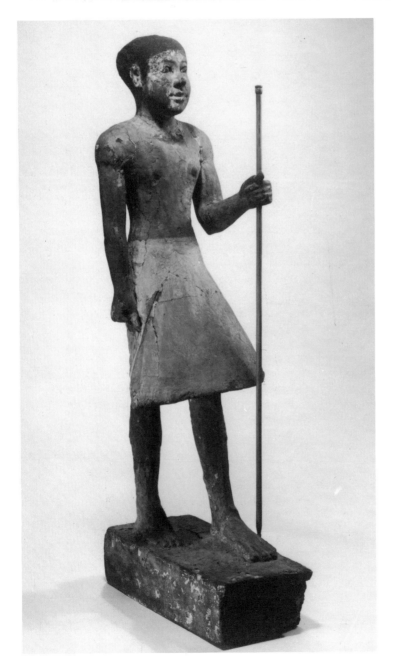

Left: An important Egyptian
figure of an official, *c*23rd
century BC. Plastered and
painted wood.

The successes start with Egyptian art, where one of the most important items historically is a censer inscribed with the name of Amaris. The provenance of the Egyptian antiquities collected by Ricketts and Shannon is unfortunately not always clear, but as there were only a limited number of sources, one of which was the auction room, more information may eventually appear about the origins of the items. Some Egyptian things are illustrated in *All for Art*, the catalogue of an exhibition of their bequests to Cambridge and London held in 1979 at the Fitzwilliam Museum. This catalogue is the most up-to-date source of information about the collection as a whole.

Clearly, the attraction of Egyptian antiquities for Ricketts was not only historical in a general sense, but partly sensuous. Writing of purchases made in 1911 at a sale in which he was generally outbid by an agent for the Musée Guimet in Paris, but obtained some incidental objects like a toilet scoop, ivory pins, and supports, he remarked, 'I have got besides quite a nest of pots and potlets of the pre-dynastic period, cut out of plum-pudding stone, collared head in brown stone, and gorgonzola marble, and a good large head of a cow in sandstone, Middle Empire said to have been found at Dehr-el-Bahari (all cows grow there now!).' It was in this year that Ricketts and Shannon made a first visit to Egypt, Ricketts was much impressed: 'I liked Sakkara but, as I thought, I arrived there tired and found the best things often difficult to see. They are full of invention and achieve a high level of technical skill, they do not however equal the base reliefs from Abusier or the reliefs in the tomb of Ramose at Thebes. I liked the Punt reliefs at Dehr-el-Bahari greatly, but on the whole the strength of Egyptian art is in the round and the sense of mass, not in base relief. I was astonished at the real art merit of all the Colossi of Luxor, Karnak and Memphis.' From these major impressions we can turn to the artists' purchases, 'Goddesses with the heads of lions, hippopotami, hawks and other engaging animals' bought for pleasure as much as their significance. Ricketts was amused by some of their possessions and jokingly described a vase with a broken foot as having suffered from the carelessness of Clytemnestra's maid. This was partly the attitude of a stage designer, to whom objects were possible stage properties, an attitude explicitly acknowledged by Ricketts in looking at Egyptian remains which had affinities with his stage sets; but besides this element, there was also the urge of an art critic and connoisseur to distinguish between invention and technical skill on one hand, and real artistic merit on the other.

The critic reappears in a letter to Michael Field about some pots from Rhodes, which Ricketts describes as 'nice,

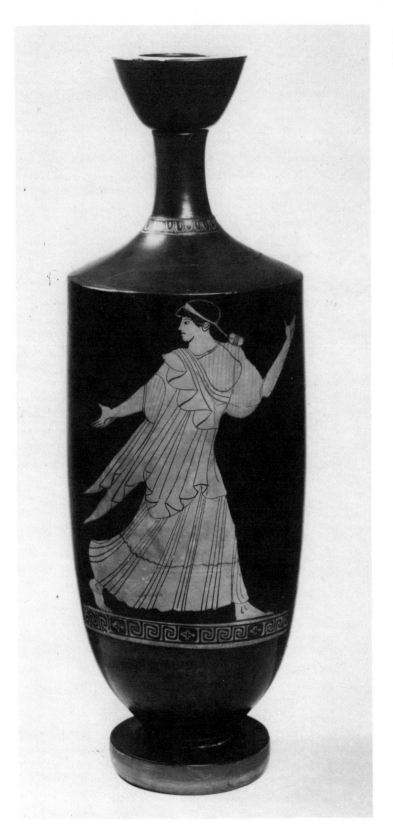

A lekythos *c*470 BC by the Berlin Painter, one of the greatest of the late archaic vase-painters.

Two Tanagra statuettes from the 3rd century BC.

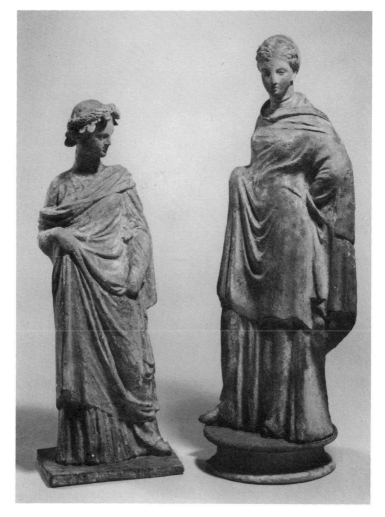

not art, but quite charming.' Qualities of art were more clearly to the forefront in his choice of Greek vases, where there was already considerable competition, although cataloguing of the field had not been started. One of the collectors in this area was E. P. Warren, a philanthropic American millionaire, who had been among the sponsors of Berenson's studies in languages and history at Oxford before he embarked on Italian painting. Warren took a house in Lewes, from where he worked, buying all over Europe and employing scholars and young men like John Fothergill to build up a magnificent collection in Boston. He was a discriminating collector, buying at the top of the market, while Ricketts was buying with difficulty at sales or, if he was unsuccessful in the auction rooms, attempting to find out prices from dealers. W. J. Ready, a dealer from whom Ricketts bought vases and other antiquities, respected his judgement enough to say that no one in London had his knowledge. Among the Greek vases in the collection,

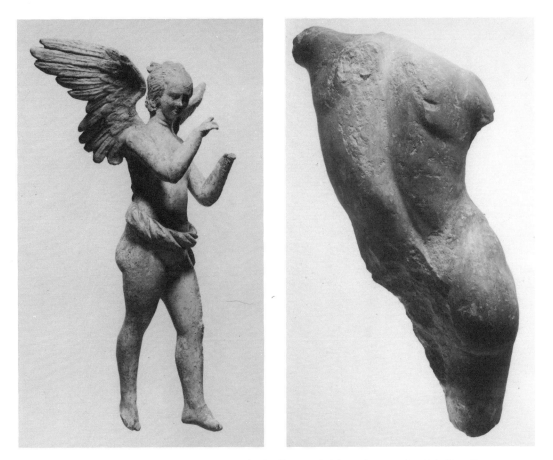

some were of the first importance artistically and historically, several of them signed. Ricketts responded to the design of Greek vases as well as their execution, comparing their quality to the design of Japanese prints. He admired Hellenistic art for its charm; the attractive terracotta figures from Tanagra shared some of that idyllic quality which had been one of the first achievements of Ricketts and Shannon as joint engravers of *Daphnis and Chloe*. Inevitably the artists bought a few fakes in collecting Tanagra figures, but an attractive group remains in the collection at Cambridge. Collecting has small ironies like the story of a Tanagra figure of an actor, which Cecil Smith at the British Museum felt unable to buy because he was not sure how the seller had come by it. He did, however, suggest the figure to Ricketts, who bought it.

Of the very few pieces of classical sculpture purchased by Ricketts and Shannon, two deserve special mention. One was a classical fragment, the only copy of a piece by Praxiteles which comes close to the original. The second is the bust of Antinous, favourite of Hadrian, portrayed as Bacchus, a late purchase for the collection when the artists were living at Townshend House. This piece came from a

Above left: Flying Eros, a Tanagra statuette from Magna Graecia, 2nd century BC.

Above right: An early Roman copy of considerable sensitivity after a lost masterpiece by Praxiteles. This fragment is the torso of Apollo, from a group in which he is shown killing a lizard. There is a portrait of Shannon with this fragment in the background.

120

Bust of Antinous, Roman, AD 130-40. This head was a late acquisition, bought by Ricketts in 1930. Antinous, Hadrian's favourite, is shown deified as Bacchus; the head was found at Hadrian's villa at Tivoli in 1769.

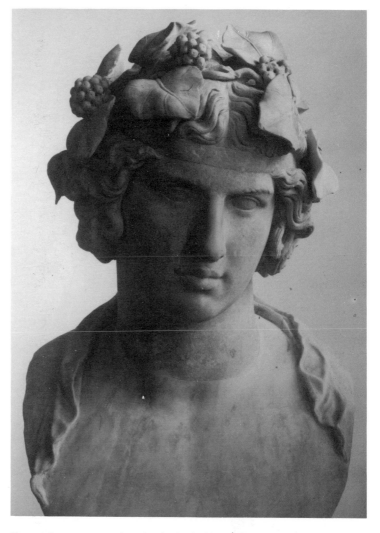

Below: Cornelian ring stone with the figure of Hermes, signed 'of Dioskourides', the Emperor Augustus' own engraver. A most important gem.

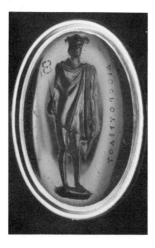

line of owners who included Sir William Hamilton the archaeologist, Ambassador and husband of Nelson's mistress.

Sculpture was clearly art, but the borderline with 'not art' is hard to define in some categories of the collection. Engraved gems were not highly priced at the beginning of the century, and perhaps the artists lost an opportunity to acquire more significant examples than they did; nevertheless there is one outstanding specimen, signed by Augustus's own engraver. Ricketts thought of learning to carve cameos, a dying art, but did not pursue the idea. The relationship of the artists' collection to their career was such that, if he had taken up the craft, they might well have formed a remarkable collection of gems. The same sort of reflection can be made about the art of other cultures. In a letter of 1920, Ricketts wrote that the war had made him 'more than ever in love with classical art, and

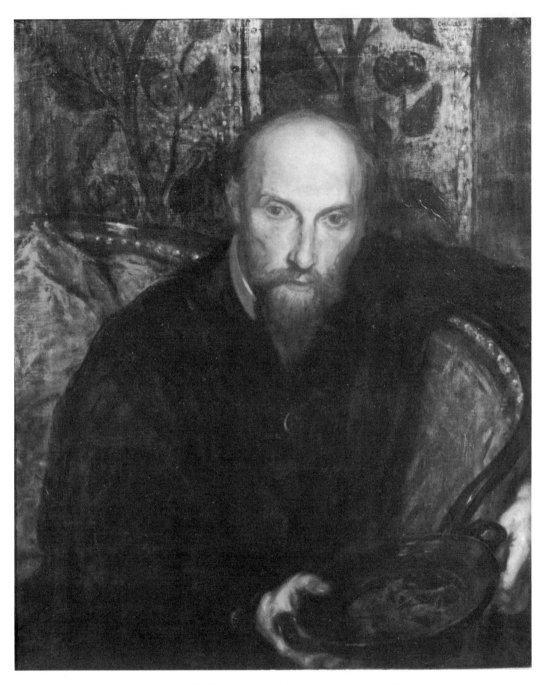

with beauty for its own sake.' He was explaining that he hoped to acquire a Benin head, and commented on pieces from the Caroline Islands as 'real *objets d'art* in colour, surface and finish.' Trying to match the unfamiliar with a known quality, he went on 'Some of the New Zealanders' objects are really interesting and make one think of Wotan and the Norse world.' We can see Ricketts wavering, sure of his liking for these other arts, but realising that they

The Man with the Greek Vase, a portrait of Ricketts by Shannon, 1916. Shannon painted both himself and Ricketts with an outstanding item from their collection.

122

were not related to his main artistic interests and his allegiance to the European tradition. The same problem facing young French artists in the 'twenties was answered by such repudiation of the European tradition that the Surrealists valued above all the strange, magical and alien elements in, say, Polynesian art. Ricketts felt the attraction, as he wrote in *Pages on Art*: 'I have a distinct liking for savage art, idols of feather, amulets of wood; a mere shell-tipped arrow conjures up the magic of distances, or the aromatic gloom of forests where a savage may crouch, watching for his prey, silent, immovable, primaeval, whilst at his side some large flower opens, fades and sinks unnoticed upon its stem. I can imagine time in the space between the unmusical cries of the tide in the coral reef beyond like distant cannon, of the sea on its return.' His liking in this case was not converted into acquisition, at least not on any important scale. The obvious contrast is with artists whose practice made them keenly interested in other cultures as points of reference for their own work, such as Jacob Epstein who made a valuable collection of sculpture, mainly from Africa, or Roger Fry and Clive Bell whose critical arguments in favour of new movements in art were backed by analogies with what Clive Bell called negro art.

The main part of the Ricketts and Shannon collection consisted of drawings, chiefly of figures, or figure compositions, first because they could afford such drawings and secondly because this branch of art was relevant to their own work. The financial limitations placed on the collection cannot easily be established. The artists' income in their early days derived from teaching, illustration and Ricketts's annual allowance of £100 from his grandfather. The Vale Press was founded with a legacy of £500 from Ricketts's grandfather, and £1000 from Hacon. Good management of the Press finances by Holmes provided welcome support. In December 1905 Ricketts recorded, 'In the last months I have sold four pictures and three bronzes, this looks as if the ice were beginning to break at last, for last year I sold nothing, I earned sixty pounds from Obach in prints of old blocks; the year before, I made fifteen pounds on two sketches; two years before that, forty pounds on a small picture, and if I had not a faculty for journalism, which so far I had not used, the outlook might have seemed black, for my nest-egg of the Vale Press is less by several hundreds.' He wrote that Shannon's reputation had increased: 'We are supposed to do very well, the last two years have been good for him, but his earnings are a trifle of what he might expect to do, compared with other less well-known artists.' In a passage concerning the war and their contributions to charities, Ricketts mentioned having £400 in the bank; the artists' finances in those difficult

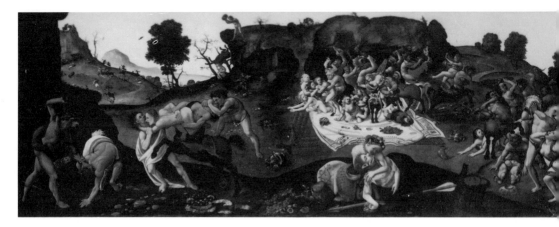

years were covered by a legacy from Katherine Bradley. Ricketts calculated that their combined incomes had rarely exceeded £1000 a year and were seldom half that. There were particular disappointments – the lack of interest from buyers in Ricketts's bronze show, the low sales of his book on Titian and the failure of *Pages on Art* to bring in much more than the cost of the typing. The result was that the artists could only rarely afford paintings.

They made an exception for Piero di Cosimo's *Centaurs and Lapiths*, which they bequeathed to the National Gallery. The painting was offered to them for £700 after having been turned down by the Louvre. It is an important picture with a quirky, individual character far removed from Shannon's pastoral and idyllic paintings, or the melancholy pictures of Ricketts. Also, it has a strong linear design which runs counter to the atmospheric and evocative effects of colour aimed at by both the artists, but its exciting subject and lively composition, as well as the sheer technical quality, persuaded the painters to make the purchase. A painting by Puvis de Chavannes, with its grave nobility was more in tune with their own artistic intentions – the painting was sold on their purchase of Townshend House but the artists retained several of his drawings. Other major paintings included a portrait of Archbishop Laud, now considered a studio replica of the original by Van Dyck in the Hermitage, but believed by Ricketts to be by Van Dyck himself. A painting even closer to their own practice (in this instance Shannon's portraiture) was the painting by Alfred Stevens of Leonard Collmann, for which they paid £300. Some more paintings were also bought to be kept. Others, as in the case of Daumier, were sold again. A great artist like Delacroix was represented by three oil sketches bought early in their career by Shannon at Christie's and not given up.

If there are some hazards in identifying the artists' taste with their purchases in general, this is certainly true of

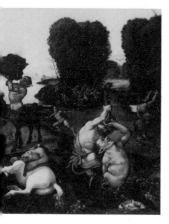

Above: The Battle of Lapiths and Centaurs by Piero di Cosimo. This masterpiece was bequeathed to the National Gallery. It was the most expensive purchase of their lives, costing £700, but rightly held pride of place among their paintings.

Right: Archbishop Laud. There are several versions of Van Dyck's portrait of Laud, the original usually held to be that in Leningrad. Ricketts thought this painting, bought 'for the price of a good frame', was the original.

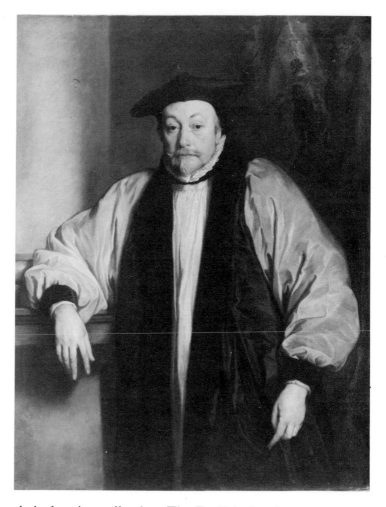

their drawing collection. The English drawings outnumber most of those representing other schools; Alfred Stevens, Burne-Jones, and Ricketts's protegé Ernest Cole make up the largest group by individual artists. The range reflects opportunity as well as personal choice – many of Alfred Stevens's drawings, for example, came from one sale (in which Ricketts and Shannon were bidding against Sir Edmund Davis), and the artists were invited to visit Burne-Jones' studio after his death, acquiring several works as a result. For Ricketts and Shannon, the attraction of Stevens and Cole lay in the power of their figure drawing, whereas their feeling for Burne-Jones arose more out of sympathy with his idealism. Burne-Jones's description of a picture might equally be applied to one of Shannon's works: 'I mean by a picture a beautiful romantic dream of something that never was, never will be – in a light better than any light ever shone – in a land no one can define or remember, only desire.' Pre-Raphaelite drawings were also well represented in their collection of Rossetti's work; there were

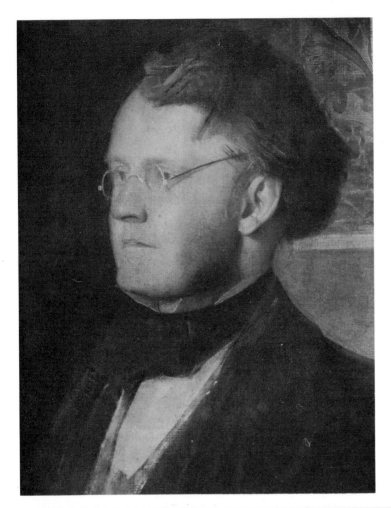

Leonard W. Collmann by Alfred Stevens. An extravagant purchase at £300, Ricketts felt that this companion to Mrs Collmann at the Tate Gallery was 'one of his masterpieces. We also understand the rumour that it resembled Shannon's painting; at its birth, Titian and Ingres stood sponsors; at the birth of Shannon, Titian and Velasquez.'

Right:
Study for a bronze group for the new County Hall by Ernest Cole, 1916. Cole's early work, especially his draughtmanship, was much admired by Ricketts, who even tried to prevent his conscription during World War I, saying, 'his loss in the trenches I would consider a national disaster.' Cole later turned to modern style in sculpture, to Ricketts' great disappointment.

Below: The Backgammon Players, Sir Edward Burne Jones, 1861. The idyllic background is taken from the garden of William Morris's Red House. The girl is a likeness of his wife, Jane Morris.

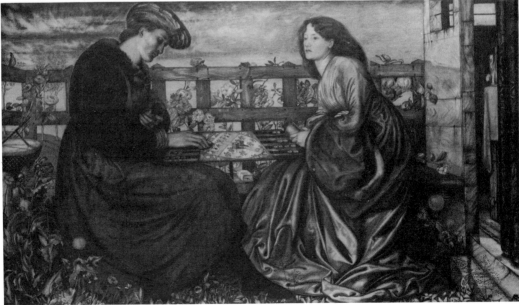

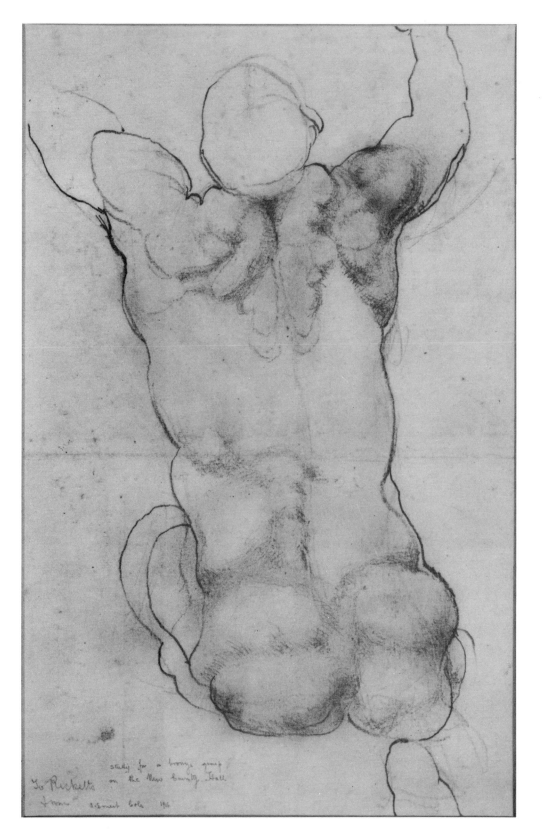

study for a bronze group
To Ricketts on the New Trinity Hall
from Albert Cole 1911

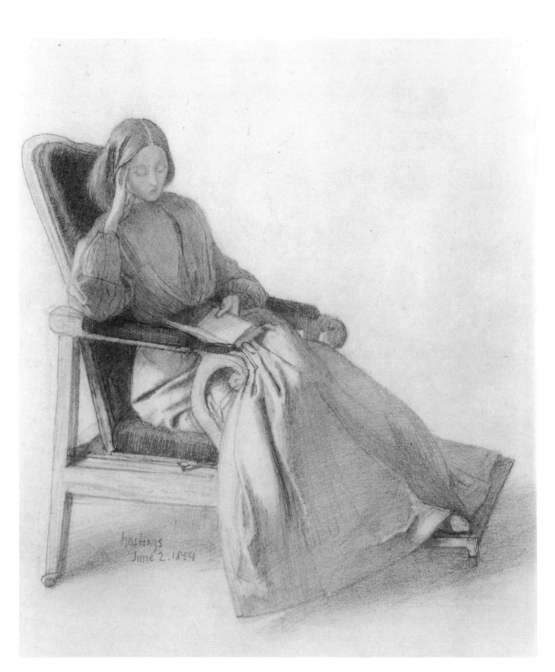

two portrait studies of Elizabeth Siddal, 'feeble in work-manship but quite exquisite in feeling', the drawing *Golden Water* which had belonged to Ruskin, and the magnificent *Mary Magdalene at the door of Simon the Pharisee*, rediscovered at a shop in the Brompton Road in 1898, after a period when it had vanished from sight. This detailed narrative drawing, composed of figure groups and full of incident, was the subject of an explicit commentary by Rossetti, from which we learn that elements which might seem simply decorative can also hold a deeper meaning. 'A farmer crops

Elizabeth Siddal, reading, a pencil drawing by Dante Gabriel Rossetti inscribed: 'hastings/June 2 1854.

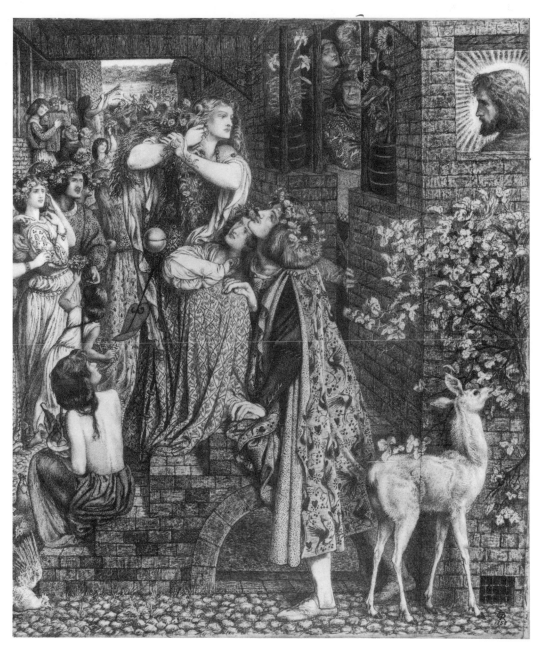

Mary Magdalene at the door of Simon the Pharisee, 1858. One of Rossetti's most important drawings with the extensive narrative allusions of his early work.

his vine on the wall where Christ is seen, and some fowl gather to share the bigger girl's dinner, giving a kind of equivalent to Christ's words: "Let the dogs under the table eat of his children's crumbs".' The drawing represents not only psychological narrative, however, but also that 'hypersensitivity' which characterised Rossetti's work and which Ricketts considered to have been derived originally from Keats.

The narrative element of some of the English drawings in the collection seems to bear out the opinion agreed by

129

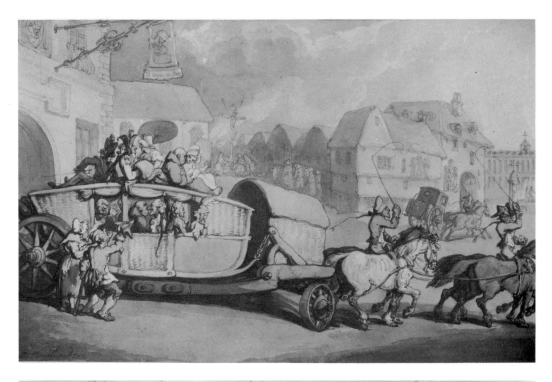

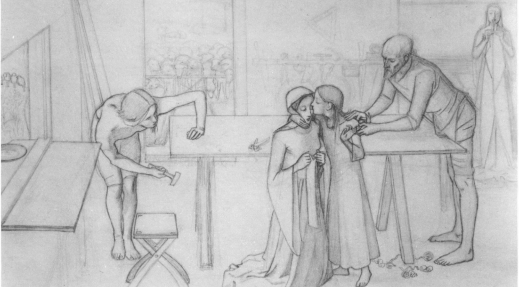

Lucien Pissarro and his father that Ricketts was essentially a literary painter, although Rowlandson (well represented by eight drawings) has more than narrative to commend his art. Studies by Sir David Wilkie and Sir John Gilbert were no more likely than the work of, say, Millais or Holman Hunt to be approved by Pissarro's Impressionist taste, nor the drawings by that enemy of the Impressionists, Alphonse Legros.

Above: Drawing by Thomas Rowlandson, *The Paris Diligence* (leaving Le Cocque en Pâte Inn).
Below: Christ in the House of His Parents, a preliminary study for Millais' famous painting exhibited at the Royal Academy in 1850, when it provoked a sharp attack from Charles Dickens.

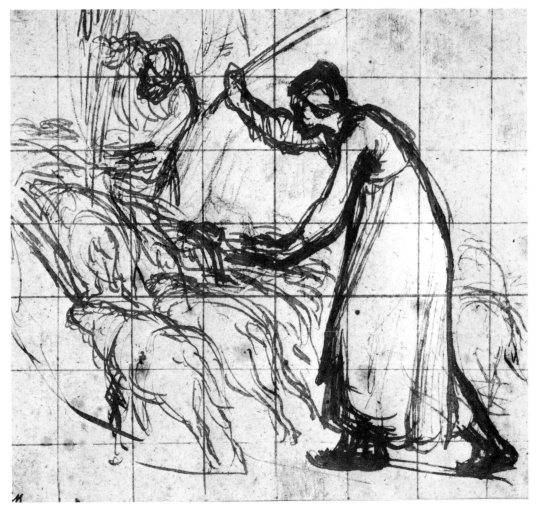

Above: The Shepherdess, a pen and ink drawing by Jean François Millet. Ricketts valued Millet's peasant women, 'Millet's bucolic temper brooded round a central woman-type; he painted by preference the woman who moulds the bread.'

Figure studies again form a large part of the artists' collection of French art, which contains drawings by some of the great names of the nineteenth century: Delacroix, Millet, Puvis de Chavannes and Rodin. Of these, especially Puvis worked in a way that was relevant to the personal style of Ricketts or Shannon. Francophile though they were (particularly Ricketts, with his fluent French and quick, Gallic enthusiams), they felt such an aversion to many developments in French art in the late nineteenth century that Ricketts was left praising an expert decorator, Paul Baudry – whose reputation had fallen so low in the 1960s that André Malraux commissioned Marc Chagall to paint over ceilings by him in the Paris Opéra. In other periods of French art, the collection reflected a general taste, and included several fine eighteenth-century drawings, notably by Watteau, but also by Lancret and Delarue. (Ricketts over-optimistically believed the Delarue drawings to be the work of Fragonard).

131

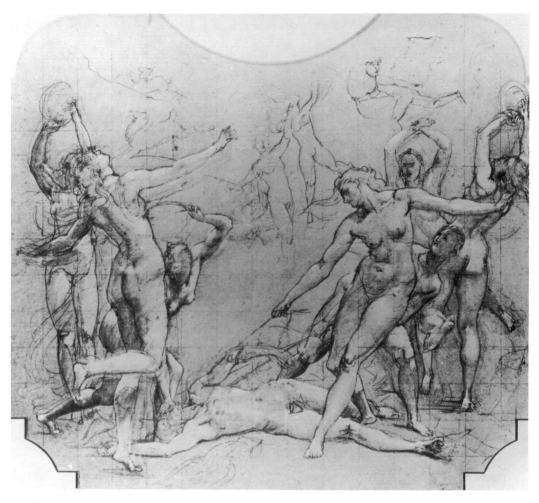

The most famous drawings in the collection however, are those belonging to the sixteenth and seventeenth centuries. A relationship with the artists' own practice is less significant here than the quality of their choices. Some of their attributions have not passed the vigorous analysis of modern scholarship, but by any standards the list of unquestionably authentic drawings is a splendid one. Titian, Tintoretto, Tiepolo, Rembrandt, Rubens, Van Dyck and Jordaens are represented by master drawings, and the quality of works by other artists is high, even when they are not universally accepted by scholars. Filippo Lippi, Lorenzo di Credi, Bernadino Luini, Guido Reni, Barocchio, Campagnola, Castiglione, Domenichino, Domenicho Fetti, Primaticcio – all these and more are to be found at Cambridge, the result of an exciting pursuit of quality, extending over forty years.

Many drawings were bought at auction and in specific cases (for instance the drawing by Lorenzo di Credi) we know both where the sale took place and the identity of

Above: Copy of a drawing by Paul Baudry, *Orphée et les Ménades,* for the Paris Opera. In 1914 Ricketts wrote in his diary 'The fall of the bomb near the Paris Opera House set me thinking about the possible destruction of the Baudry ceilings, which I value more than I can say.'

132

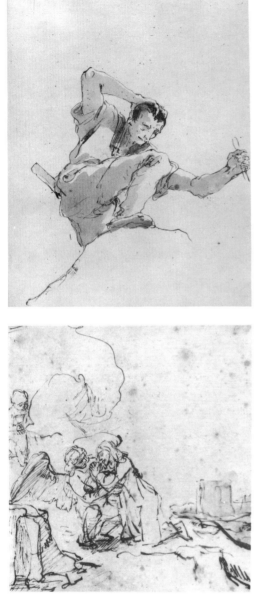

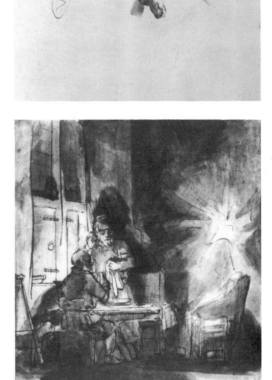

Opposite, top left & right: Two drawings by Giovanni Battista Tiepolo; study of a man climbing and study for a female nude, seated on clouds.

Above: Two drawings by Rembrandt, prized possessions of the two artists; *left: The Agony in the Garden,* and, *right: The Supper at Emmaus.*

the previous owner. The provenance of other drawings is sometimes difficult to trace: We can tell only from a reference in Ricketts's diary that the fine group of drawings by Tiepolo was obtained by means of an exchange with Sir Edmund Davis. The attribution to Titian is a particularly important piece of connoisseurship, but then Titian's rare drawings (to which Ricketts devoted a chapter of his book on the artist) were for him an especially important topic. One drawing in the collection, a fragment of a child, considered by Ricketts to be the work of Lorenzo di Credi, underwent a change of attribution after a visit to the artists

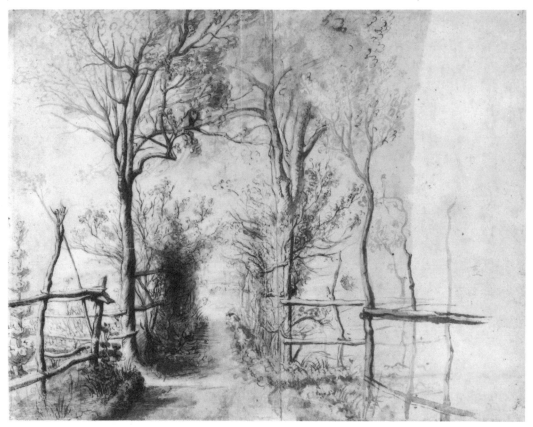

by the Swedish scholar Osvald Siren, who agreed with the
opinion Shannon had already formed that it was the work
of Leonardo, producing photographs to support his theory.
The fragment entered the Fitzwilliam collection under the
name of Leonardo, but has since been deprived of this
status and given a safer attribution to Verrocchio.

Since Berenson's livelihood depended on his attributions,
he was the object of numerous jokes. Ricketts once suggested that the closure of a Belgian museum had taken
place in order to prevent Berenson from making any more
attributions. His opinion (though welcome, no doubt, when
he approved of the attribution to Masaccio of the small
roundel now relegated to the Florentine School) was not
perhaps treated with the seriousness Berenson felt his due.
In his account of a meeting with Berenson's patroness,
Ricketts sums up the difference in their attitudes:

'Met Mrs Gardner of Boston, the famous collector. I was
told she was seventy and rather difficult. I found she looked
forty-five, and carried herself well and was singularly frank
and charming. I sat next to her and we soon got away from
the commonplace of recent events and vague art talk into
pleasant squabbles about nature and religion. She goes to
Nature for consolation. I view it as a drama or story –

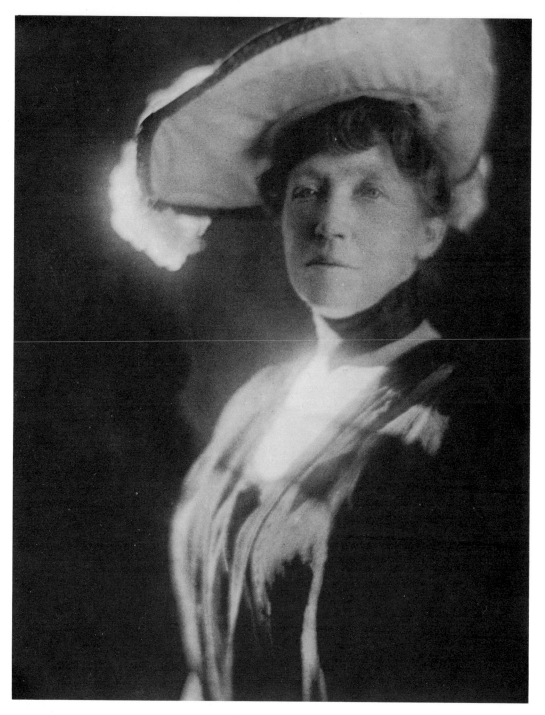

Mrs Isabella Stewart Gardner.

telling picture book. Our host got mean and tried to correct our bad tendencies to admire Rodin and be interested in Richard Strauss. Over some stupid matter of attributions he said, "But Ricketts and I always disagree, we see in opposites." I said, "Oh no, my dear Berenson, you are not so wrong as all that, sometimes you are quite right".'

Oriental Art

Ricketts and Shannon were among the most informed connoisseurs of Oriental art in England from the late 1890s. Shannon was a keen buyer of Japanese art, in which he took a particular interest – Ricketts noted in his diary that Shannon's energy had doubled their oriental collection during 1913. Laurence Binyon, the poet and playwright – and

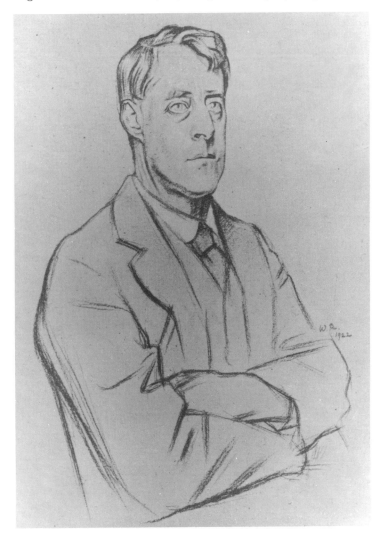

Laurence Binyon by William Rothenstein, 1922. As well as being a poet of distinction and a playright, Binyon's writings on art included *Painting in the Far East*, a pioneering work at the time of its publication in 1908.

oriental expert at the British Museum – was a constant friend. His catalogue of the Japanese and Chinese woodcuts in the museum, published in 1916, is one of the most sustained works of oriental scholarship in the period. Binyon was responsible for a request for advice from Ricketts on the quality of the museum's collection, rather to Ricketts's dismay, since he had to explain to Binyon's superior, Sir Sidney Colvin, how poor much of the material was. Binyon's efforts were instrumental in improving the collection, and Ricketts was persuaded to write about oriental art – one of his articles was subsequently reprinted in *Pages on Art*. Ricketts and Shannon kept the needs of the British Museum in mind as collectors and left the main part of their collection to the museum. It was an important and valuable bequest, especially strong in the work of several major artists, including Harunobu, Utamaro and Hokusai, whom Ricketts and Shannon much admired.

The attraction of Japanese prints was primarily aesthetic. In 1900 Ricketts wrote in his diary, 'I think, at their best that nothing quite touches a first-rate Jap print, excepting a good Greek Kylix or a first-rate Tanagra: even the latter hardly compare: only the masterpieces of the greatest masters go beyond: picked Titians or Rembrandts, or world-famous frescoes.' That was a collector's view, but as an artist he also liked the specific qualities of design and technique in which Japanese prints often excelled. In addition Ricketts, with his sharp eye for fashionable decoration and dramatic effects, made specific use of his observation when he was asked to dress the D'Oyly Carte production of *The Mikado*, though his costume designs throughout his career owe something to Japanese examples in their breadth of effect.

Ricketts was much influenced by the writing of Edmond de Goncourt in his assessment of Japanese art. Goncourt's excellent books on Utamaro and Hokusai were landmarks, describing the narrative content of the most important prints, and outlining, say, the scope of Hokusai's illustrated books. Goncourt skilfully evoked the charm of another world in his passages about Japan. He wrote poetically of life in the *Maisons Vertes*, the geisha district of Edo, and the charm of the figures and their occupations, combining his description with a discriminating account of the quality of the particular prints he had seen. His was the voice of a collector, talking with pride about his own possessions and a tinge of envy about other people's. Binyon, with the British Museum catalogue, Charles Holmes, with his monograph on Hokusai and, indeed, Ricketts and Shannon in the development of their taste in Japanese art are all indebted to the two books by Edmond de Goncourt.

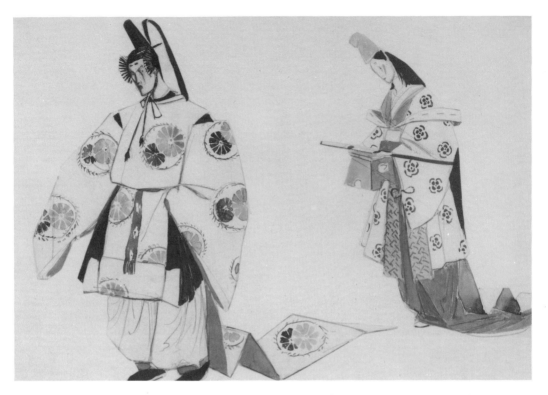

The artists' enthusiasm for Japanese prints had begun in their student days. On winning a prize, Sturge Moore bought prints that he knew Ricketts and Shannon wanted, but could not afford, instead of buying books for himself as he was expected to do. By 1897, they had the confidence and resources to make one of the great hauls of their lives, buying at auction works from the collection of Captain Brinkley that included Hokusai drawings, some of which were reproduced in Holmes's book on the artist a year later.

In the 1890s Japanese prints were cheap. As this popular art was still thought unimportant in Japan, the major collections were formed in Europe and the United States. Despite the existence of such collections as that amassed by Vever or Gouse, there was every possibility for artists like Aubrey Beardsley or William Rothenstein to make acquisitions. Ricketts and Shannon bought some prints from galleries, but also turned to the sources used by dealers, seeking out a furniture dealer from whom van Wisselingh had bought prints. Llewellyn Hacon had a collection of Japanese prints, including some by Harunobu which Ricketts and Shannon later acquired. By the end of their lives, they owned more than 350 Japanese prints, to which may be added oriental drawings, as well as some precious Persian examples which were sold to help pay the costs of Shannon's illness.

Ricketts' designs for costumes for *The Mikado*. Ricketts recorded that Binyon was overwhelmed with the success of these costumes done for the D'Oyly Carte production, for which they are still in use.

138

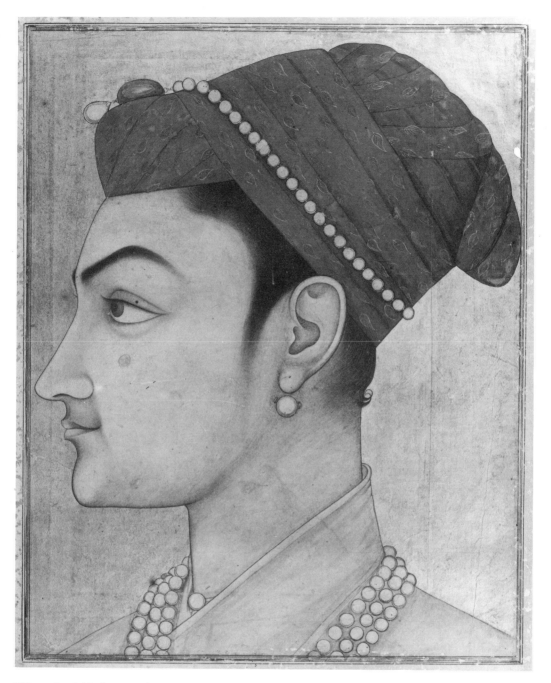

This magisterial Indian portrait from the 17th century was one of the few remnants of the Persian and Indian art owned by the two artists – Persian drawings were among those sold to pay for Shannon's medical expenses.

There was some interest in oriental art in London, but in Paris much more. As early as the 1850s, Felix Bracquemond had been the moving spirit of a Japanese Society, and prints were on display at the *Exposition Universelle* by 1867. For the rest of the century, artists adapted Japanese ideas to their paintings. Manet, Degas, Van Gogh and Bonnard (who was referred to as the very Japanese nabi) were all influenced by Japanese art, while Whistler was remarkably successful in adapting a Hokusai composition for his picture of Battersea Bridge.

Fashionable taste had already overtaken prices in some oriental ceramics by the turn of the century. As a young man, Whistler had admired and collected blue and white porcelain, a taste that was shared by Wilde and Rossetti, but the sort of hawthorn jar which Whistler had bought in the 1860s was able to fetch several hundred pounds by the 1890s. Economic facts of life therefore dictated that Ricketts and Shannon seek pieces for their collection among less costly examples of oriental art. In the event, they only occasionally bought such things as screens or modern Japanese *objets d'art*. Their purchases were prized for their own sake and, filled though their homes were with possessions, they remained rooms which held a collection, rather than fashionable or artistic interiors. The distinction becomes clearer in contrast with the environments created by Roger Fry and his friends. Fry's Omega Workshop was intended to undertake whole interiors with the artist's touch evident throughout the entire room in murals, furniture, ceramics, fabrics. Ricketts might choose objects for pleasure, Shannon might design furniture or a fabric but their work was always meant to combine with the beautiful, strange, amusing or delightful things that they owned in a demonstration of their idiosyncratic and eclectic taste.

The Japanese scholar Kohitsu reacted to their collection with interest on a visit to London. Ricketts first mentioned their acquaintance in a diary entry of 1902. '[Binyon] told me that the hereditary expert of the Shogun family is now in England, studying Greek art. He knows three words of English and five words of French. He expresses dislike only by gestures and spitting sounds. He was shown some of the kakemonos and verified some signed guarantees of authenticity by his father and grandfather. He raved with admiration before *Sage Crossing the River on a Sword* by Motonobu and the *Hotei with Children* by Sesshiu.'

After meeting Kohitsu, he commented, 'He is younger than I thought, more pink than usual with Japanese, the eyes inscrutable. He still finds our painters indistinguishable, but is interested in Rembrandt and Rubens drawings. He has also been vastly impressed by Persian and Rhodian pottery, and by Tanagras to a small extent.' When Kohitsu visited the painters' collection, he seemed intently alive and interested in most of the things he saw. 'He looked at all the Tanagras with keenness, but did not seem really interested in the Greek pots, which I think he thought curious and mostly like lacquer. He behaved like a child when we gave him some Greek beads, and was greatly and I think genuinely interested in the Persian paintings. He discovered and liked the little cup by Zeshin: his father

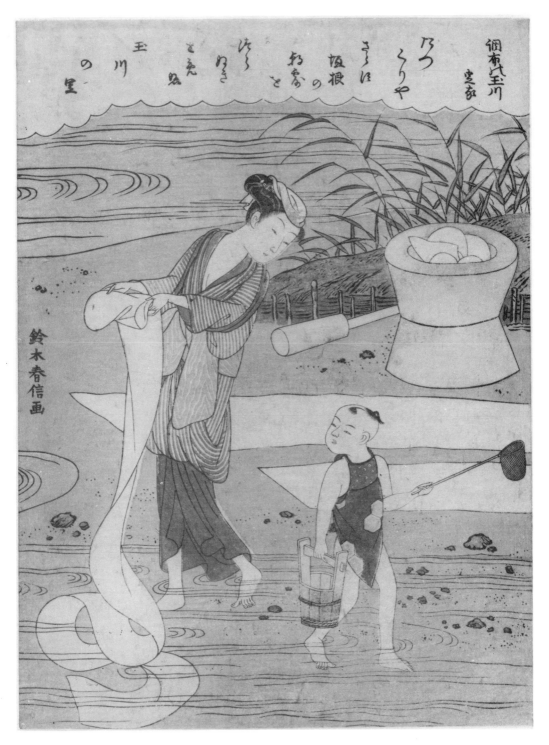

調布玉川
定歌

ぬの
さらす
さらは
坂根
の
お多か
と
沒へ
ぬさ
と
名
玉
川
の
里

鈴木春信画

Suzuki Harunobu, *Woman with boy carrying fishing net*. This important early master was particularly well represented in the collection.

had known him when a drunken old artist. He told us a story of Zeshin liking work only when it brought in money – money for *saké*.'

In talking to Kohitsu, Ricketts had '... the delightful

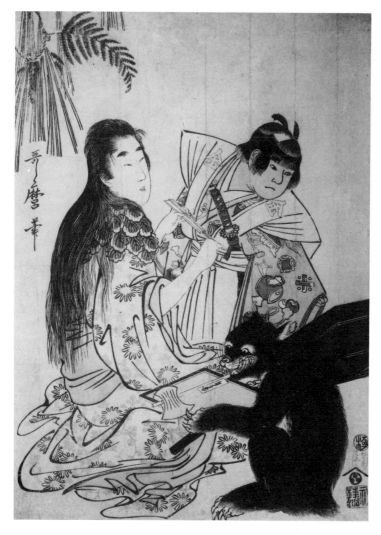

and stimulating experience of trying to give an idea of the
sequence and proportionate importance of the great European makers to a Japanese student of the art of his own
country... Under his questions the strain put upon my
habitual admirations was not unlike that which a man
might experience were an angel to question him about his
beliefs, or the reason for wearing our modern clothes. I felt
bashful at times about the art of many masters, and some
nations even, whilst the greatness of some famous Japanese
seemed to him almost too difficult to convey.' Part of the
difficulty of communication was the appeal of obvious qualities to European eyes, the attraction which led to European collecting of the popular prints.

Ricketts tried to avoid the temptation to stop at the
immediate attraction of Oriental art, although he felt he
lacked the expert knowledge which could view rare things
in relation to the ideals they expressed. Some art he found

uncongenial, such as the animal caricatures of the early Japanese scroll attributed to Abbot Toba Sojo, but the sense of design apparent in the work of Korin made him for Ricketts one of the most notable artists in the history of that world. 'Were I to say that he reduced facts to symbols of their qualities or aspect, I should merely describe what has been the case with all early Japanese painting. Such a definition does not take into account the pattern making element in his work, which ignores the imitations of fact, and at times sets a wholly arbitrary value on experience. His work astonishes and charms; daring, yet sure of itself, it is alert and strong. Perhaps a phrase of his expresses his purpose better than any clumsy attempt at definition. These are his words: "I wish to feel that I am a prince when I paint." It is characteristic that for Kohitsu Korin focussed certain tendencies, doubtless in a splendid way, yet with an emphasis which seemed sensational to his taste and altogether delightful to me.'

Ricketts's relish for Japanese art is clear in his writing on several major print-makers. The attraction of Harunobu must partly have been historical – the knowledge that he stood at the beginning of a development in colour block technique, still with influence in the present. Shannon, like Lucien Pissarro, was professionally interested in colour prints, and made some successful experiments in this field.

It was, however, in writing about an artist like Utamaro that Ricketts was at his best. In *The Dial* in 1897 he compared the artist with Botticelli and the Italian Renaissance, and cited Tanagra figures in comparison with Utamaro's gracefully posed women. Ricketts sensed a possible criticism of Utamaro's scope and quality, 'A feeling that, with this Japanese, a monotonous and even feminine bent of mind make an infinite refinement in form and colour, but may lead many to suspect him, and with him the whole eighteenth century art of Japan.' Ricketts, however, was prepared to defend the fact that 'The spirit in which Utamaro designed has affinities with aristocratic and aesthetic conditions,' and went on to express delight in the quality of Utamaro's prints. 'Print after print reveals his quest after delicate line and rare colour harmonics. He will select from the fleeting graces of a game, or from the motions of reverie alike; all this he will clothe with the tints of early flowers and leaves; his mere paper will be mottled with traces of colour that has been removed, or glazed with a frosted substance like faded silver. He possesses to the full the resources of a colourist who is always sensitive in the matter of surfaces – the colourist of a country which has several names for white.' Finally, on an almost directly personal note Ricketts added 'The all-absorbing, the gluttonous melancholy at the heart of the East, touches Japan

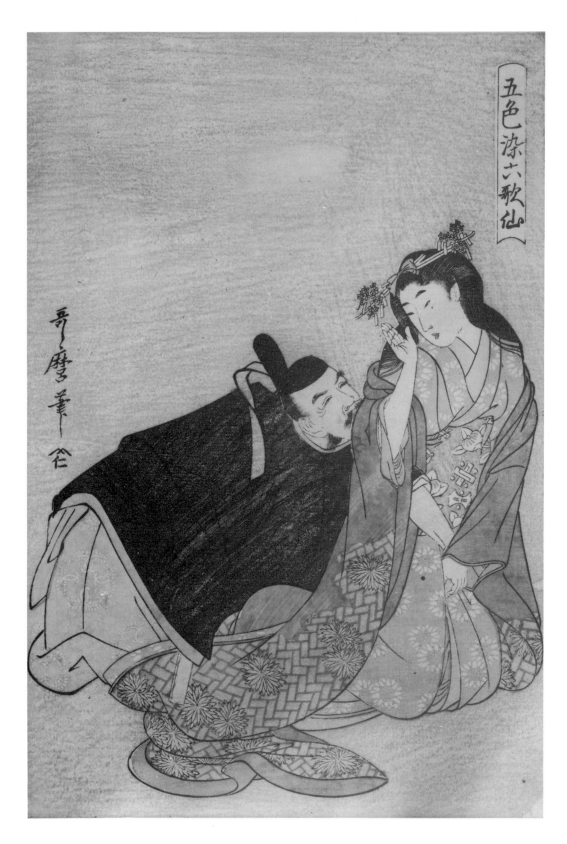

but little; they are apt to be ironical about it, to pass it by in a verse or a simile with a gaiety which is foreign to us also, or at any rate to recognising it nobly, as the passion for the few. One of their greatest artists, Utamaro, has accepted these conditions, ministering exquisitely to the needs of an audience that to him was never dull and rarely tired. A great sense of perfection alone makes that finer sadness from which all sense of perfection is seldom entirely free.' In a memorable phrase Ricketts felt Utamaro leads us into 'charmed spaces.'

The charm of Utamaro did not blind Ricketts and Shannon to the realist gifts of Hokusai whom Ricketts felt was underestimated by Japanese taste, although he conceded that Hokusai may have drawn too much. But 'He has rendered the silence of snows and of immemorial peaks and the life of flowers; the laughter of a child moved him; so did the melancholy of the warrior leaning on his lance and the sweep of restless seas.'

The opinions expressed by Holmes in the book on Hokusai, written at Binyon's suggestion, reflect the views of a group of friends and admirers of Japanese art. The relatively low regard in which Hokusai was generally held at the time called for defence by Holmes. 'To claim a place among the great masters for an oriental artisan, unrecognised even by connoisseurs of his own country, may therefore seem to convict the claimant of caprice, if not of wilful

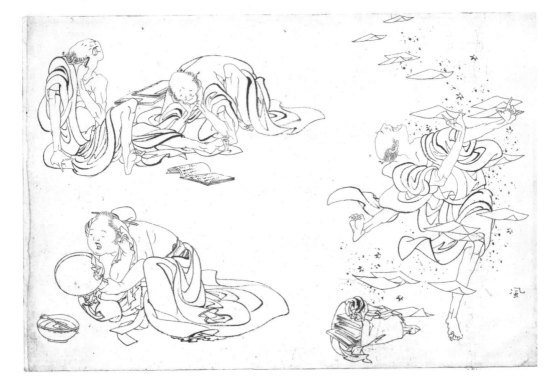

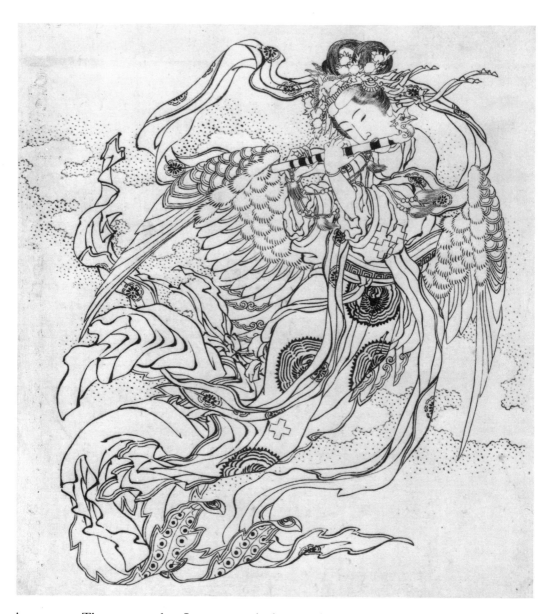

ignorance. Those unused to Japanese paintings and colour-prints are apt to pass them by as mere curiosities, interesting perhaps but only one degree less remote than the carved monsters on a Polynesian war-club.' Holmes emphasised the characteristics in convention, such as the absence of shadows, that distinguish Japanese art from European painting, and preclude 'the pretentious realism that would make a picture a kind of sham nature.' He sought rather to identify Hokusai's skill with that of Rubens 'His touch, smooth, unerring, includes in its easy sweep men, women and children in every state of motion or rest, noting affectionately those instinctive, momentary gestures which make action natural.'

The Goddess Kwannon. Ricketts and Shannon believed this drawing to be by Hokusai himself, and Holmes included it in his book on the artist. It is now described as belonging to the School of Utagawa.

Right:
Potted pine, bowl of water and guto by Hokusai. The high standard of wood-block colour printing and the effects obtained by Japanese artists was of great interest to the artists, who experimented with various techniques themselves

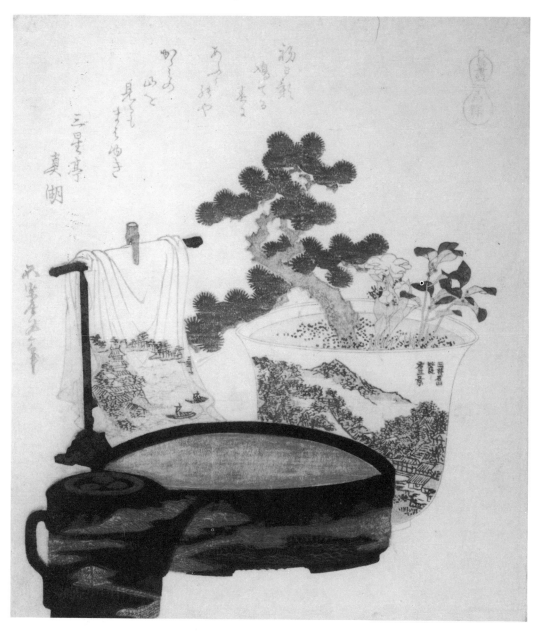

Overleaf, above: Hokusai. One of the artist's views of Mount Fuji, with a water wheel as the prominent motif. A similar composition (with a bridge in the foreground) was used by Whistler as a basis for his *Battersea Bridge*.

Below: Utagawa Hiroshige, *The First Tokaido number 30. Hamamatsu.* There are relatively few later prints by artists working after Hokusai in the 19th century.

Beyond the gestures of historical and cultural sympathy which Ricketts and his friends made towards oriental art, beyond their technical appreciation (especially of prints), there were, ultimately, sensuous responses to be made. In a passage reminiscent of Pater's famous praise of the Mona Lisa, Ricketts writes of the attraction of things once bright which have been dimmed by the handling of time. He admits that, in Utamaro's prints, 'Time and use have dimmed the stronger oppositions of blacks and yellows, violets and crimsons, or the vivid crossings of white used to freshen any languor of effect, and have given an added

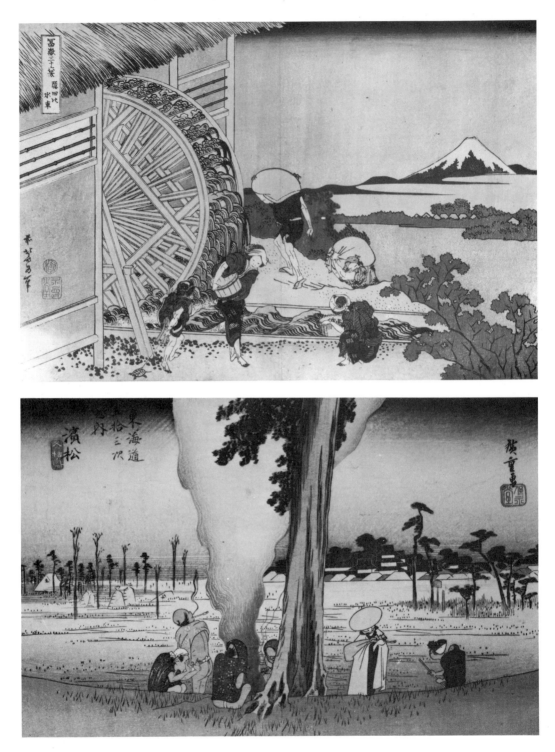

subtlety that cannot be found in new colours or surfaces, make his effects more rare and his colours more grave: but this is but an added charm to that which was beautiful from the first.'

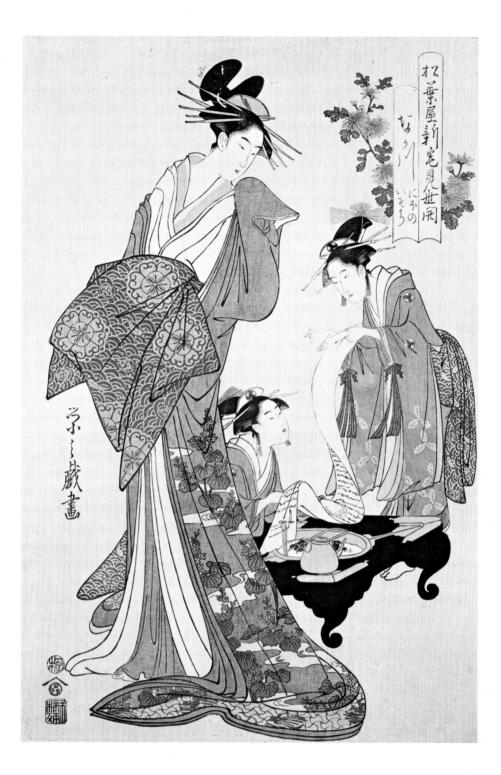

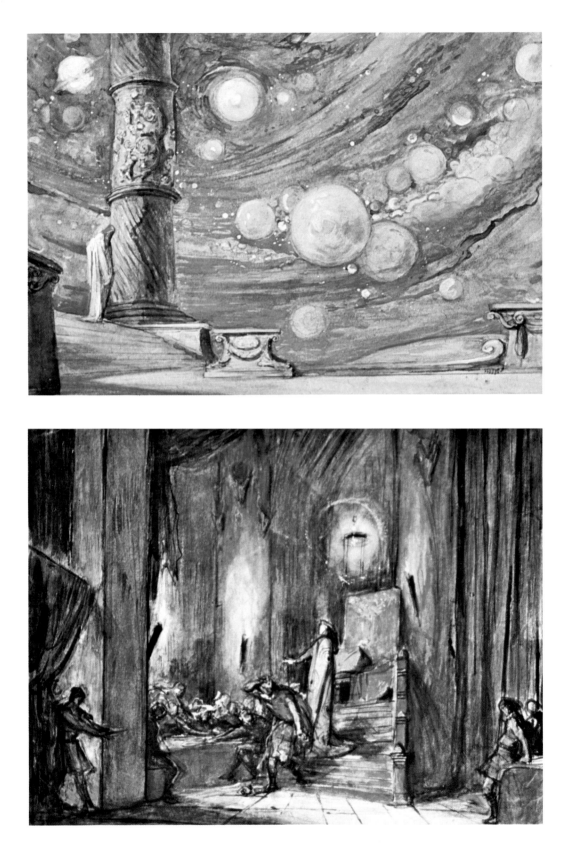

The Art Adviser

Ricketts's connection with the National Gallery of Canada began in 1923. His appointment as adviser was formalised in 1927, and until 1931 he was active in recommending and commenting on purchases for the gallery. His advice was valued highly and, at his death, the Director of the National Gallery, Eric Brown, wrote to Mackenzie King.

'He was a very great artist in many ways and a very charming and companionable person. No one living had a greater sensitiveness towards the forms of art he particularly appreciated and few ever possessed greater knowledge of subjects he chose to make his own, such as 15th and 16th century Italian pictures, old master drawings, costume of all ages, Japanese prints and drawings and everything to do with the arts of wood engraving, fine printing and stage design. His connection with the National Gallery for six years was a very happy one, full of pleasant memories and many interesting discussions, and I am very regretful it has come to an end.'

Ricketts himself was pleased with what he managed to achieve for the National Gallery. He felt that 'In Venetian pictures of the 16th century Ottawa already compares favourably with the Metropolitan of New York despite its gigantic financial resources.' He also made a point of the impression made by an Ottawa picture at the Italian exhibition at the Royal Academy in London in 1930 – 'Our Tintoretto is greatly admired by all the pundits.' This picture, known as *Tintoretto's Servant* was one of the prized purchases of Ricketts's career as an adviser, although some other acquisitions were arguably more important – several of them obtained through private generosity rather than from public funds. At this period Eric Brown was having difficulty in establishing a proper level of government backing for the gallery, and it was one of Ricketts's merits that his personal advocacy and reputation helped to stimulate both private benefactions and public money.

Brown's first aim in persuading Ricketts to be the gallery's adviser was to take advantage of his expertise and

Left, top: Ricketts' design for the set for the Epilogue of Cecil Lewis's *Montezuma*, c1920, a play which was never staged. *Bottom:* Ricketts' stage setting for the Banquet scene in *Macbeth*, staged at the Prince's Theatre in 1926.

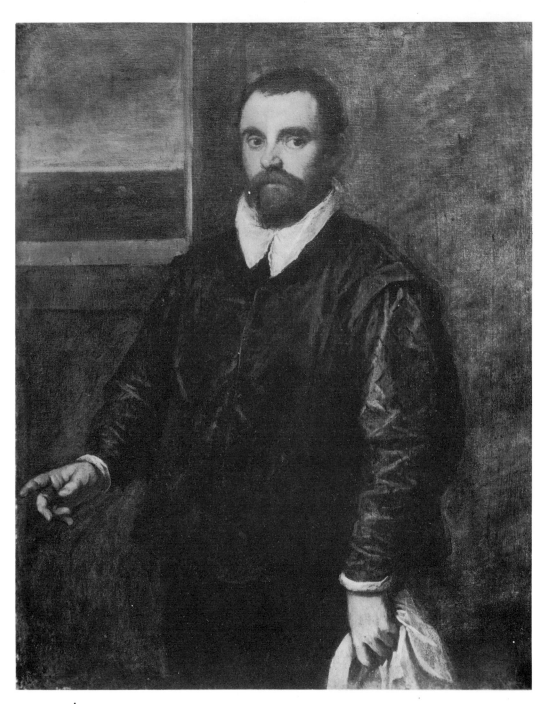

knowledge of the market. Brown referred to both Ricketts and Shannon in correspondence with the Chairman of the gallery's Trustees, Sir Edmund Walker – 'I believe we should get some very good bargains, their taste and knowledge is exceptional and with an actual incentive to buy, I am sure they would do even better than they do now.' It is evident, however, that Ricketts was the main agent in

Tintoretto's Servant. In a formal letter written to help Brown, Ricketts wrote 'This picture by Tintoretto is not only a superb work of art, it is unique in character in the output of the master in its singular blend of homeliness and dignity.'

152

business. His letters to Brown occasionally mention Shannon's support for some proposed purchase, or some doubt in his mind: 'A very serious careful darkened half length portrait by Rubens was bought by Durlachers last season, I wonder if this is what you have in view. I valued it greatly. Shannon remained cold but it needed cleaning.' In another case he wrote, 'The Stubbs, *Death of the Doe*, turned up at Christie's more than a year ago. Shannon suggested its purchase to E. Davis for his country house. Davis (as usual) did not budge. Poor Aitken, of the Tate, put £150 on it (he has no funds) but lost it to Agnew who purchased it just under £200 I believe. It is priced £300 but I think, for Canada I might get it for less. The picture is about 4 feet across, in its old 18th century frame. The landscape is entirely brown, the figure and animals rather hot in colour. There is a vague Chinese look about the work which is very careful in execution and in perfect preservation. It is a curiously attractive and unexpected early work . . . Shannon is solid for the picture, against it is its size possibly? No, I favour it greatly, it is intensely English in temper.'

Brown was sharply aware of difficulties in the art market in the 1920s. In London there were relatively few dealers, and only a handful of important ones. Prices were exceedingly high in some areas of collecting, notably eighteenth-century paintings and furniture of an aristocratic kind, partly because of the skilful and successful sales policy of Lord Duveen. Italian Renaissance painting was one of the most difficult classes because of difficulties in the attribution of pictures. Duveen was fortunate in having the advice of that expert on Italian pictures, Bernard Berenson. The National Gallery of Canada was poor, having at its disposal only £7,000–£10,000 a year for its purchases. Ricketts was a realistic buyer. In writing about the market he commented, 'In the sale rooms from £200 to £400 often obtains something better of its kind than £1,000 where you touch a level of excellence where competition is keener . . .' On policy, he felt that purchases were, in a sense, more difficult for a small gallery than for a rich and big one. 'They should be highly characteristic or very typical of their kind, and against this is the high rate of values. Certain schools and masters are practically unobtainable, and a definite and sequent policy daily more difficult.' He commented in 1926 that the huge prices obtained at Christie's for such English artists as Romney possibly represented 'speculation in fashionable values.' In considering the purchase of a portrait by Reynolds he remarked, 'I like the Reynolds of General Halimand immensely from the photograph: of its kind it seems almost first rate, but the price ("about 5 thousand guineas") is excessive. The market value of a

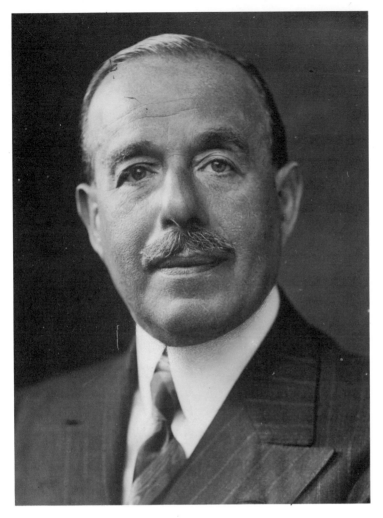

man's portrait of this size is between two and three
thousand.'

Ricketts was scornful of many of the pretentious attributions put forward by dealers, who frequently lobbied the
Canadian gallery. 'The "Vermeer" – by some anonymous
Dutchman – was priced £35,000, the Turner (possibly a
Paul) about £1,000. I forget the price of the Gainsborough
which was a sound commonplace work of the Beechey type.
This dealer will probably end in gaol.' After seeing a prized
collection, he wrote, 'His collection is very varied but con-
fined to damaged pictures of uncertain authorship which
centuries of collecting have left on the Italian market.
Everyday in London similar darkened and damaged pictures pass through Robinson and Fisher and the Monday
sale at Christie's.' As well as discussing prices with Alec
Martin at Christie's, Ricketts kept in touch with a number
of dealers; Colnaghi's and Durlacher were firms from which
purchases were made; so, too was Agnew's. He knew both

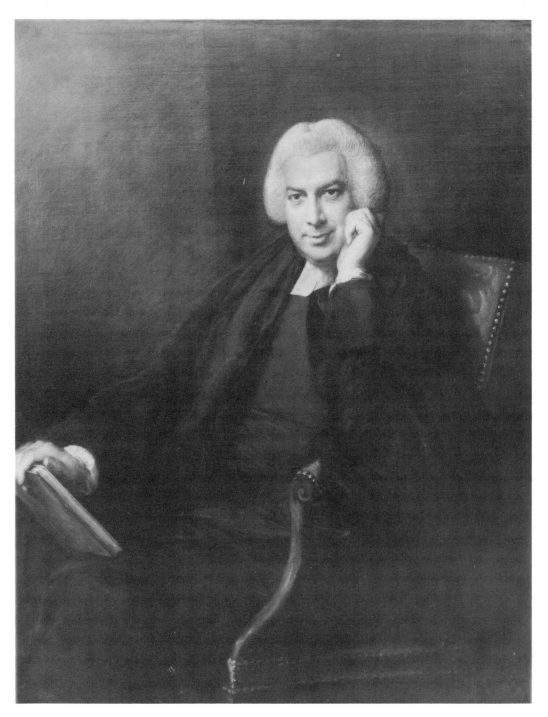

The Reverend Stephens by Gainsborough. A rare purchase in the expensive English 18th century market.

Colin Agnew and Carstairs of Knoedler well, and in investigating the possibility of obtaining a picture from the Holford collection, one of the great collections to be dispersed at that time, he wrote to Brown 'I suppose you could not get anyone to present a Holford picture to your gallery? I could probably square Carstairs and Colin not

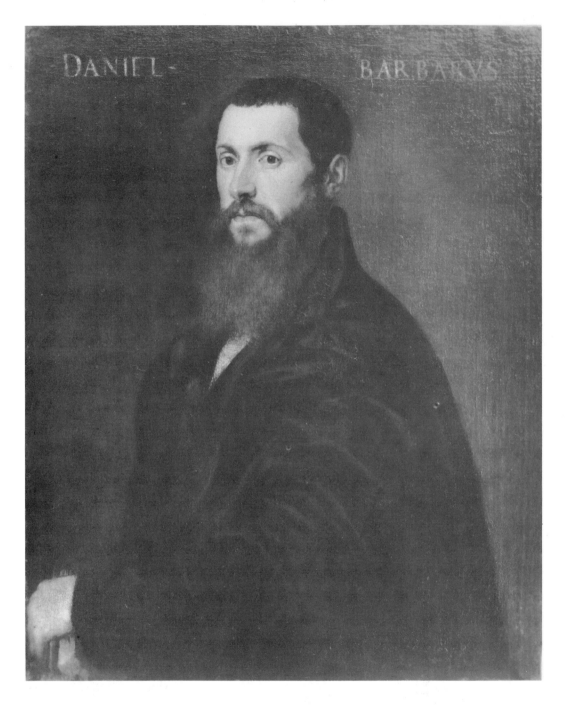

to get in the way. The first might be grateful for tips on several works.' In some instances Agnew's sold directly to Brown. Ricketts wrote of a Titian which Agnew's were to take to New York, 'Colin has discovered a bad senile Titian of the kind one would have rather left undiscovered,' only to hear in return 'I expect Colin Agnew will be over in October and probably he will have his Titian with him. I

Daniel Barberus by Titian.

156

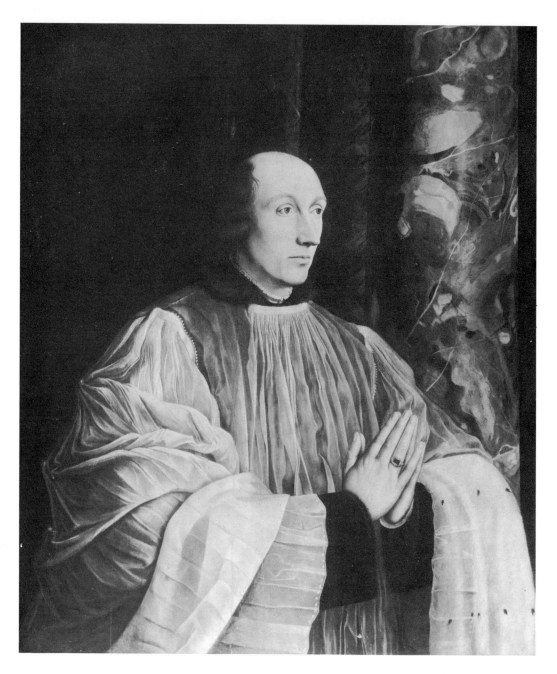

Georges d'Egremont, Bishop of Utrecht. A painting given to the Gallery by H.S. Southam, one of the group of rich Canadians with whom Brown was building up good relations for the Gallery.

am already sure that his opinion will *not* coincide with yours.'

In general, Brown and Ricketts worked satisfactorily together, though not without some disagreement over prices, especially when they both had a hand in a purchase. They both saw the 'twenties as a time of opportunity for the gallery, because of the number of sales being made, and united to make the best of the chances offered. A typical comment indicating Ricketts's constant awareness

157

of the market is that 'It will be good people being tired of hanging on.' One of the main difficulties in building up the collection was how to effect major purchases once they had decided that a work was of special significance. A possible long-term answer to the problem of money – the formation of a society similar to the National Art Collections Fund in Britain – was only under discussion while Ricketts was adviser. Another solution was to find patrons who were prepared to donate the money for a particular purchase. The most important of these gifts was a painting of the penitent Magdalen by Van Dyck presented by William Southam, to which Ricketts reacted warmly 'I will write to Mr Southam to congratulate him personally. Such generous acts cannot be too highly praised. They are not given the importance they deserve.' Another significant gift was a portrait believed to be of Georges d'Egremont, Bishop of Utrecht, then attributed to Jan Provost, which was presented by H. S. Southam, William Southam's son. H. S. Southam was one of several benefactors whom Brown had interested in a National Art Collections Fund: 'H. S. Southam definitely promises £1,000 a year for the next five years and we are moving to get a group of his friends equally financially strong to do the same or more if possible.' The New York stock market crash put a stop to progress.

A painting which Ricketts thought especially suitable for the gallery was a portrait of a man in a red coat by Perronneau, an artist for whose work Canada was vying with London, 'Within the last few weeks the National Gallery has been glad to accept a very poor and unrepresentative Perronneau.' In 1977 the value of this painter's work was reaffirmed by a very beautiful picture acquired by the same gallery. Fifty years or so earlier, Ricketts had written, 'Perronneau is greatly to the fore in the art collecting world in Europe, being the new star in the firmament of the French school.' He was pleased when Brown succeeded in having the picture presented by the heirs of Sir Edmund Walker: he felt 'From the big museum point of view it is the most outstanding or exceptional purchase of the year, though I fancy the Rubens and Piombo will prove the more valuable purchases from the point of view of the general public.' When he came to look at the picture after treatment, he was very much disappointed with its condition: 'The tragedy is the Perronneau which I consider ruined, the glazes have gone and it looks very inferior to the Davis portrait.'

A third method of obtaining pictures which the gallery could not buy from its purchase fund was by special grant, the first of which in Ricketts's period as adviser was for Veronese's *Magdalen*, one of the gallery's great pictures. A

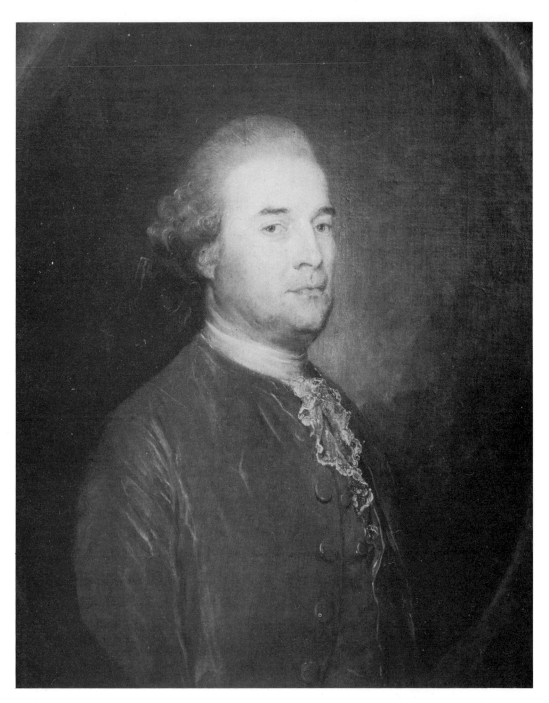

Man in a Red Coat by Perroneau. Sir Edmund Davis owned a fine painting by Perroneau, with which this picture was compared.

number of paintings were considered from the point of view that, as key works, they would help to establish the fame of the gallery, but were rejected for different reasons. One was a portrait of Pitt; another was Van Dyck's *Rinaldo and Arminda*, although 'I would not advise the sinking of your yearly allowance for a space of years, though the work in the matter of artistic merit, rarity and historical importance

159

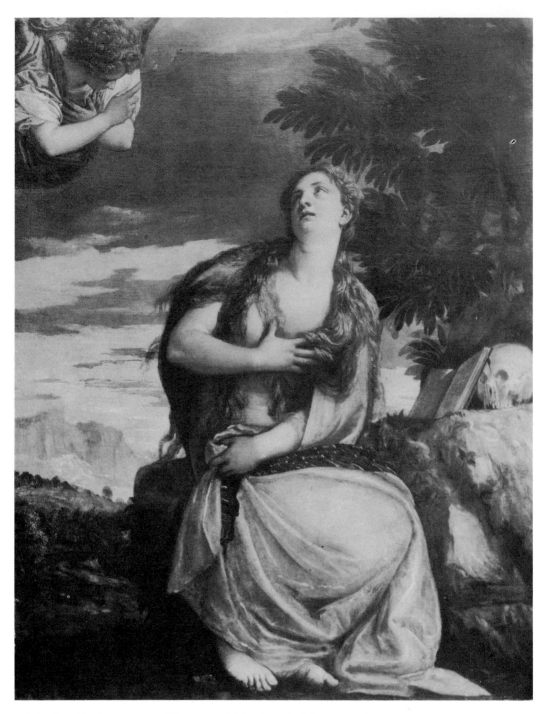

Veronese's *Magdalen*. A special grant was made to the Gallery for this outstanding picture.

might justify the course. There would be inevitable general difficulties to manage this and you would deprive a young gallery of its annual acquisitions during the rapid dispersal of works now going on.' A third slightly comic episode was the possibility that Christie's were going to dispose of a portrait by Gainsborough of their founder. Brown dis-

Ricketts made more than one attempt to purchase pictures by Canaletto for the Gallery (on one occasion he misjudged the prices and advised putting £2,000 on a picture which fetched £6,000). This admirable picture, *The Piazzetta, Venice*, was one of his successes.

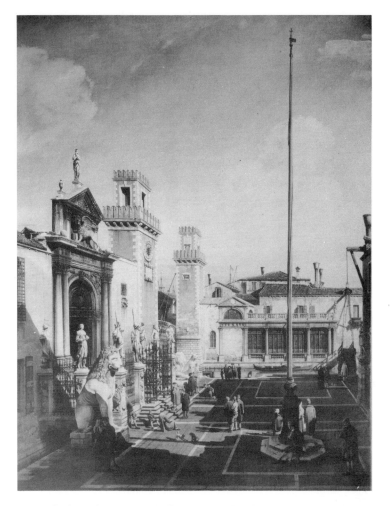

cussed the picture with Ramsay MacDonald, who was in Canada at that time and spoke at an occasion to promote the building of the new gallery (though the building had not been completed in 1979). Ramsay MacDonald characterised it as a disgrace that the firm should part with the portrait, and so it would have been. A special grant was successfully requested for paintings by Canaletto. Ricketts realised what an asset they could be. 'Should an extra grant be necessary I should put it on the Canalettos, as one is one of the best known, and the slogan that Ottawa would then rank second to the National Gallery in one of its outstanding features should have weight.'

It was the problem of money which led Ricketts to extend his advisory work in Canada. As Ottawa's recurring lack of funds meant that possible purchases had to be turned down, he accepted a second post as adviser to the Toronto art gallery. One of his actions there was to persuade Duveen to take back a picture. Since Duveen was clever enough to tell stories against himself, it is no surprise to find Brown writing, 'I hear Duveen repeats his old story of last year whenever your name is mentioned, so he evidently has not got over the return of the Wood picture yet.' In the previous year he had written of the gallery's director, 'Frank Wood has had no difficulty in exchanging the Titian and in its place has the *Daedalus and Icarus.*'

As well as acting for the National Gallery of Canada in London, Ricketts travelled either alone or with Brown in Europe. He paid only one visit to Canada, when, in 1927, there was a possibility that purchases might be made for Ottawa from the Benson collection, which was particularly rich in Italian Renaissance pictures. Ricketts enjoyed his visit. He found Canada 'a very beautiful country, well wooded, with picturesque hills, lakes, and noble rivers, a touch of Scotland but more spacious.' He worked hard, and ate well to make up for it, though not all the food was to his European palate – the blue point oysters had an india-rubbery taste, and he disliked the clam: 'It tastes of wet retriever dog.' However, Canadian trees were a pleasure, maple, elm and 'the scarlet oaks which have huge coloured leaves.' His feelings about Canada's eastern cities were muted. 'Quebec under Scottish mist, looked like Scotland, with railway station, Baronial, mixed with sordid houses!' 'Montreal is not bad, half American half Scotch, good shops of the Selfridge type, smartly dressed people.' It was in Toronto that he formed his most favourable impressions of Canadian life, for although he regarded it as a provincial city he liked the care taken over the university and its graduates' art education. More than this,

Opposite, left: Lord and Lady Willingdon. Ricketts took a great deal of trouble over a request for a banquetting tent from Lady Willingdon – the design and stencil-cutting took several weeks.

Opposite, right: William Lyon Mackenzie King, the Canadian Prime Minister from whom Ricketts succeeded in obtaining firmer support for The National Gallery of Canada.

Below: A city view of Quebec, with the Château Frontenac Hotel in the centre.

Below right: McGill University, Montreal. Ricketts approved of Canadian universities, particularly liking these university buildings which showed 'evidence of care and interest in new life.'

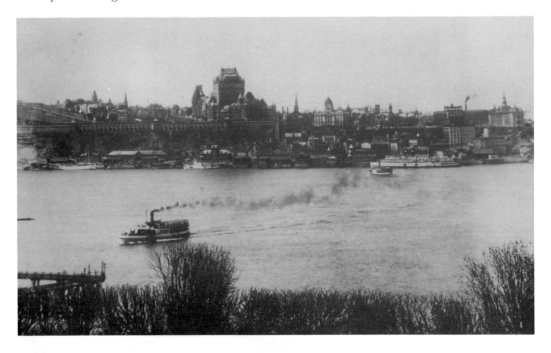

he felt a sense of Canadian energy in Toronto. 'I feel I have left the pack behind and am in the future; even here England seems to be fast asleep.'

Ricketts intended to be in Canada for nine days but spent three weeks, visiting the Van Horne collection in Montreal and meeting Lord Willingdon, the Governor-General, and Mackenzie King, the Prime Minister, key

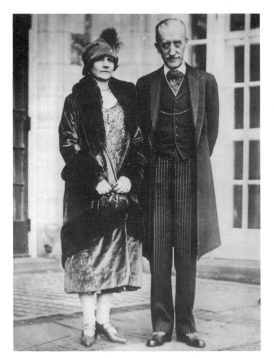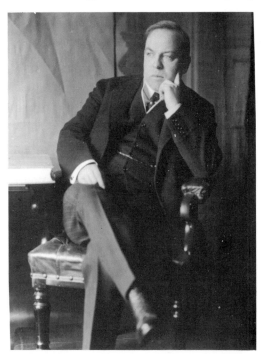

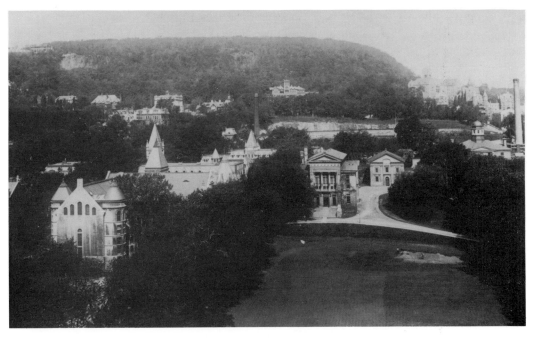

relationships affecting the future of the National Gallery, in which he was skilfully diplomatic. He described his meeting with Lord Willingdon in typical style: 'I was taken there in a glittering car all ebony and rock crystal, ushered in by flunkeys like Roman Emperors, and plunged into the first act of a West End play, with beautiful young men covered with orders, with blue silk facings to their coats (Order of St Patrick uniform). I felt I looked like Robinson Crusoe fresh from his island!' But Ricketts was more at home when he started to talk to Lord Willingdon about the future of the National Gallery and the importance of suitable Trustees. He could speak with insight about the National Gallery in London, where Charles Holmes had just resigned as Director because of difficulties with his Trustees. Lord Willingdon was impressed and repeated, 'You are the man to talk round the Prime Minister.'

Ricketts set out to fascinate the Prime Minister, and succeeded. Mackenzie King agreed to an emergency grant of £10,000 for purchases from the Benson collection. Unfortunately, the pictures wanted for Ottawa had already been sold or reserved, but Ricketts's efforts were not lost. It was vital for the future that the gallery's national importance should be recognised, that Trustees (who had thought that a grant of £10,000 would be impossible) should be encouraged. Subsequently it became easier for Brown to find supporters for his purchases and his policies.

From Canada, Ricketts went on to the East coast of the United States. He was particularly interested on visiting the Frick collection, the Gardner collection and the Metropolitan Museum, by their Egyptian and Greek antiquities, and Japanese art. He felt that ' . . . in matters of common taste the Americans are going ahead of us . . . I am conscious of a vitality and wish to do well in the Americans, and even the Canadians, which contrasts with our English indifference and apathy and the frowstiness of France.' In this comment he was referring mainly to museum displays, but he was also impressed with the energy of American collectors, thinking that it could be used in the future as a spur in persuading the Canadians to a firmer commitment to their own gallery.

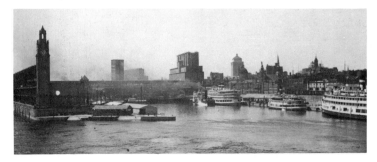

A last view of Canada, Montreal Harbour.

The Stage

Ricketts's essay on stage design appeared in 1913 in *Pages on Art*, and was dedicated to Bernard Shaw. The artists' close relationship with the theatre had lasted from their friendship with Oscar Wilde in the 1890s and was to continue until the last ten years of Ricketts's life, when he did important designs, including the D'Oyly Carte production of *The Mikado*. To a list of more than fifty productions with which Ricketts was concerned can be added costumes requested by a number of acting friends, whether or not he was to design the whole production, and many designs for projects which were never carried out.

Ricketts was strongly influenced in his designs for the theatre by developments in Germany, where productions were organised on a grand scale that required comparable buildings and facilities. An important factor was Wagner's principle that the whole audience should be able to see and hear from any angle in the amphitheatre. Ricketts was attracted to his grandiose, open and all-encompassing designs, which reflected the highly-charged quality of his music. Further influence came from the work of Alphonse Appia, whose ruling idea Ricketts praised as a 'simplification of the motives of scenery.' He heeded Appia's recommendations on the design of scenery: 'This should be broadly massed, since the actors complete the picture; over all the ever moving mystery of light and shade should be thrown to brighten or reduce the sense of reality; all fussy lighting must be avoided, since this would reduce your non-realistic scenery into mere canvas and paint, as we see it today in the pseudo-realistic settings of our melodramas and Shakespeare revivals.'

He approved of these general principles because they were in accord with his own practice, but modified them by accepting particular originality in individual temperaments, singling out Bakst for praise. Ricketts had been delighted with the settings of the Russian ballet. 'M. Bakst's enchanting stage decorations, for instance, are but the highly and very temperamental handling of conditions which are newer in result than in aim; in their non-realism alone they can be said to belong to the new art of stage decoration . . . The field he has explored is that of "fantastic decoration" and that is as vast as fancy.'

Ricketts went on to describe his own unrealised scheme for staging Oscar Wilde's *Salomé*:

'Here is my scheme. I proposed a black floor – upon which Salomé's white feet would show; this statement was meant to capture Wilde. The sky was to be a rich turquoise blue, and across by the perpendicular fall of strips of gilt matting, which should not touch the ground, and so form a sort of aerial tent above the terrace. Did Wilde actually suggest the division of the actors into separate masses of colour, today the idea seems mine! His was the scheme, however, that the Jews should be in yellow, the Romans were to be in purple, the soldiers in bronze green, and John in white. Over the dresses of Salomé, the discussions were endless: should she be black "like the night"? Silver, "like the moon"? Or – here the suggestion is Wilde's – "green like a curious poisonous lizard"? I desired that the moonlight should fall upon the ground, the source not being seen; Wilde himself hugged the idea of some "strange dim pattern in the sky".'

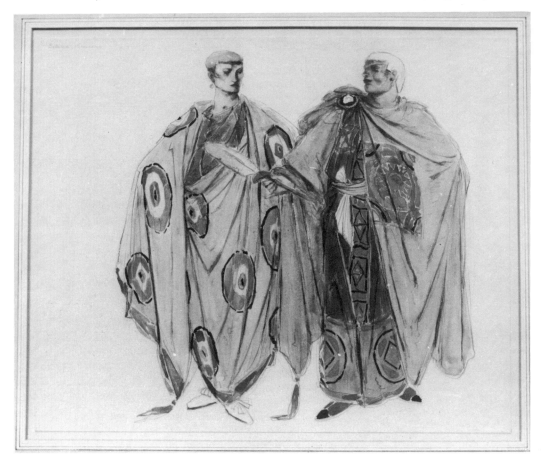

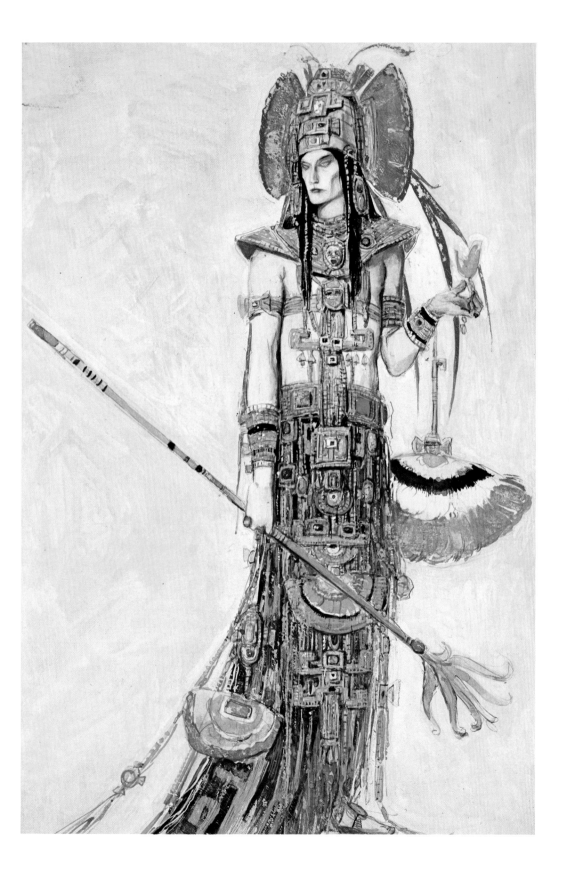

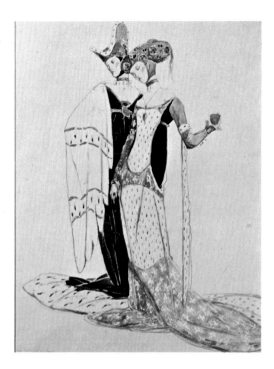

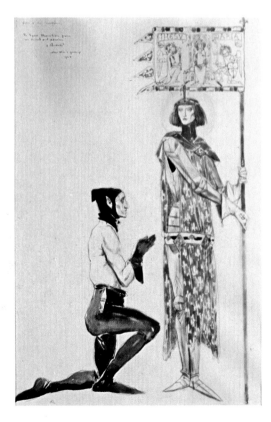

The force of such an artistic presentation was not easily accommodated in the contemporary English theatre, and Ricketts's powers as a designer in the 'nineties echoed his description of Wilde as a dramatist 'latent rather than actual.' Ricketts believed that in Wilde were lost 'The possibilities of one of those strange, complex blends in character such as Heine, for instance, whose influence is incalculable. Heine was a cynic and a sentimentalist, often a rare genius.' Ricketts speculated that Wilde might have become a great critic, or revived comedy – that 'criticism of manners and character.' He understood that Wilde had given a verbal self-portrait in Lord Illingworth in *The Ideal Husband*. Before he was released from Reading Gaol, Wilde asked to see Ricketts, who tried to rally his spirits by. talking about theatrical projects. It was too late. Ricketts was left to regret that only in his last work had Wilde given 'a hint of the power of thought, sardonic insight, and a wit that characterised the man himself.'

The actual staging of Wilde's *Salomé* was the second production of the Literary Theatre Society in 1906. The inspiration for founding this society had been the Irish Literary Theatre of W. B. Yeats, and the main supporters were Sturge Moore and Laurence Binyon. Ricketts gave the proceeds from the sale of a Vale Press book, Marlowe's *Faustus*, towards the financing of the club. Those involved in productions included Granville Barker as a director, Robert Farquharson and Lewis Casson as producers, while Bernard Shaw was among the club's supporters. In his journal, Ricketts spelt out some of his difficulties. The designs had to be achieved with an outlay of almost nothing – Granville Barker's play *The Miracle* was staged for £15, and *The Persians* by Aeschylus for £32. The acting was not good in the first production, Sturge Moore's *Aphrodite against Artemis*, but despite difficulties a Wilde double bill of *Salomé* and *A Florentine Tragedy* was a success – Robert Farquharson made an admirable Herod. Eleonora Duse went to see *Salomé* with the idea of including the character in her repertoire, but for Ricketts the main result of the club's efforts was the impact his work made on Shaw, who insisted on Ricketts as designer when he directed *Don Juan in Hell*, and *The Man of Destiny* for the Royal Court Theatre – 'Half the fun and interest of the exploit would be gone for me if it were done without you.' Discouraged by the unfavourable reception of *Salomé* in the press, Ricketts was uncertain about his name appearing as designer, but he was persuaded.

The relationship with Shaw was a cornerstone in his theatrical career. He did designs for *The Dark Lady of the Sonnets*, in 1910, also making suggestions for the incidental music. In the following year he designed costumes for the

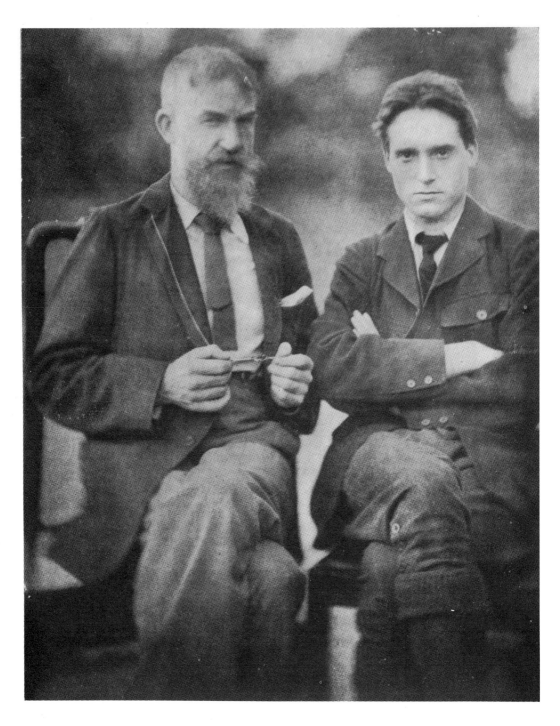

Induction and Epilogue of *Fanny's First Play*, which sur-
prised both author and designer by being a financial success. Ricketts refused to charge for his work, considering
the dresses the 'natural neighbourly act of one art to another.' His habitual trait of generosity, from which many
individuals benefited, was one of the reasons that prompted

Above: George Bernard Shaw
with Harley Granville Barker
*c*1902, two important new forces
in theatre in the period before
World War I.

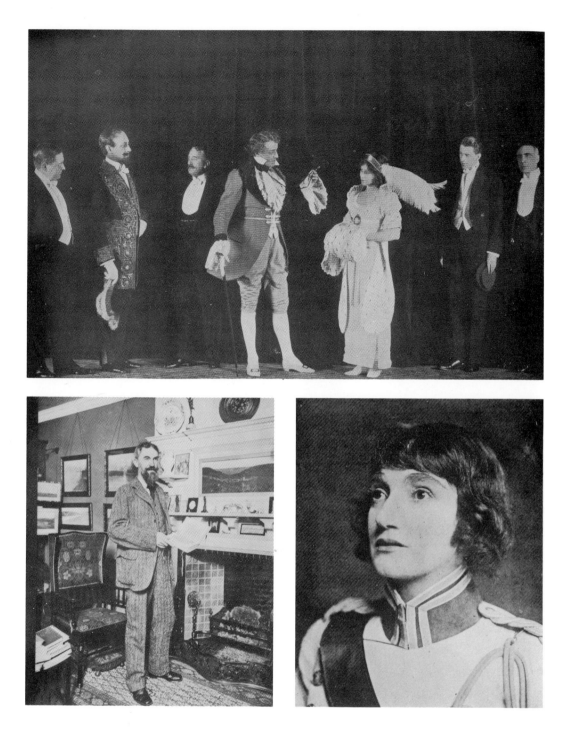

Above: The Epilogue from
Fanny's First Play, 1911.
Left: Shaw. *Right:* Lillah
McCarthy as *Annajanska, the
Wild Duchess,* 1918.

Shaw to praise Ricketts as always acting *'en grand seigneur.'*
In 1918 he did *Annajanska.* The elegant uniform that Lillah
McCarthy wore as the heroine inspired an excellent observation on male costume, 'The secret of male attire is perfect
cut worn with negligence.'

The most important of the Shavian designs was, how-

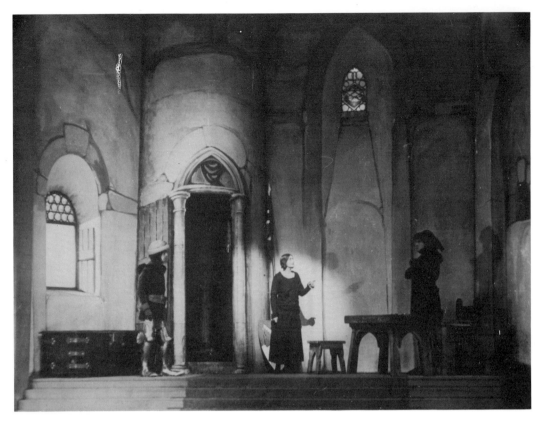

ever, the remarkable *Saint Joan* of 1924. Historical plays were directly in tune with Ricketts's abilities. For *Saint Joan*, he used the kitchen at Chilham Castle as inspiration for the first scene, achieving outstandingly beautiful effects

Above: Sybil Thorndike in the title role of *Saint Joan*, Scene I produced at the New Theatre, 1924.

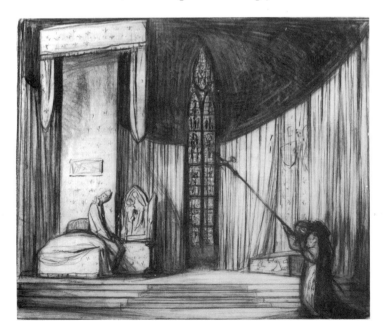

Left: Ricketts was a master of splendid effects achieved with modest means, but when he had occasion for elaboration he seized it. His theatre work was not merely decorative; as can be deduced in this drawing for *Saint Joan*, he was alert to the ways in which his setting could add to the dramatic tension of a performance.

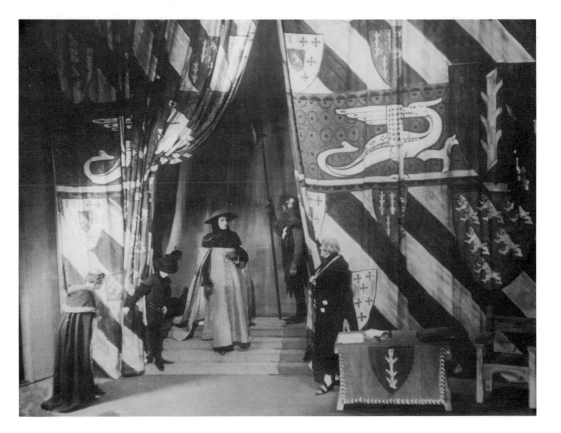

The Earl of Warwick's tent in
the English Camp, Scene IV of
Saint Joan.

with small means. Shaw was rather daunted by their splendour: 'Mr Shaw came on to the stage and said, "Scenery and clothes have ruined my play. Why can't you play it in plain clothes, as at rehearsal? Sybil is much more like Joan in her ordinary jumper and skirt than when dressed up like this, with her face all painted." ' A change in Ricketts's opinions indicates that a measure of friction had arisen between them — 'He was a sympathetic producer in the old days. Today he only thinks of his points and, I believe, dislikes good acting and production.' But the success of *Saint Joan* was balm for slight wounds, and Shaw was delighted with the publication of his text in an *édition de luxe* illustrated with Ricketts's costume designs.

The immense care that Ricketts took over historical settings and costumes, is clear from a letter requesting information from a friend about Henry VIII:

'I have to stage *Henry VIII* for Xmas and intend putting Holbein on the stage. I went yesterday to Hampton Court, but the Great Hall was shut for repairs to roof, and I was cut off from Wolsey's arms, badges, tapestries, etc . . . I believe his shield is black and gold, but do not know if his two pillars device and his crossed keys are gold or silver. Could you without inconvenience to yourself make a rough

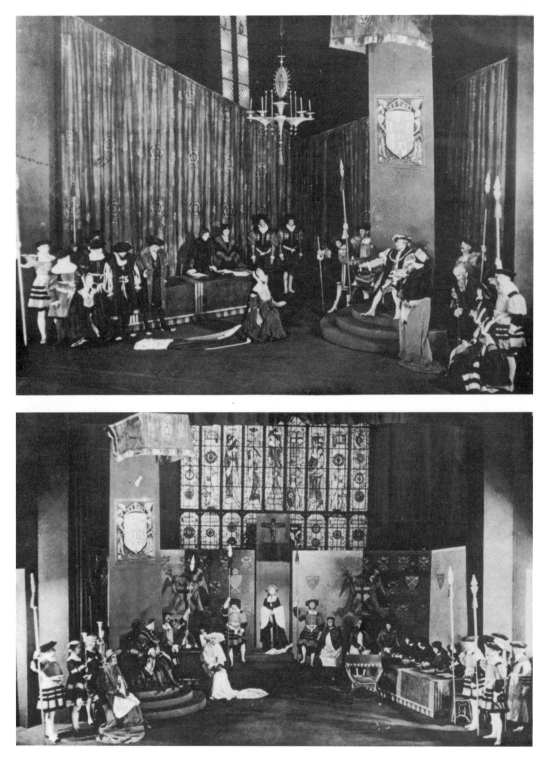

pencil outline of Anne Bullen's device and shield, panelled
with the Royal arms? I believe they exist in King's College
Chapel, Cambridge. I believe Queen Elizabeth was keen

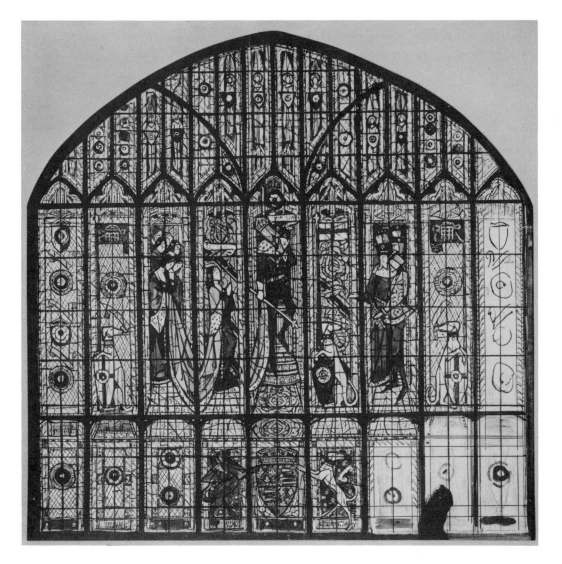

Left: Two scenes from Shakespeare's *Henry VIII* designed by Ricketts for the production at the Empire Theatre. The lower picture shows the realization of the drawing for the backcloth above.

on this vestige of her mother's royalty and, I think I am right, adopted her device, a crowned dove (?) from this. Anything bearing on Catherine's arms with England and Anne Bullen's arms would be useful to me. Don't go in for heraldic jargon – I hate it!' Given the details he needed, he was meticulous in his use of them. Sturge Moore commented, 'Some thought he wasted time on details that could not tell, but he realised they added a sense of more to see, which is like bloom on fruit to stage effect. He knew how to drive accents of historical costume farther in the same direction, so as to make them effective at a distance. For colour, pattern and cut, his designs were pre-eminent.'

Ricketts himself carried out many of his costume designs. He worked particularly hard on the production of John Masefield's mystery play *The Coming of Christ* at Canterbury

175

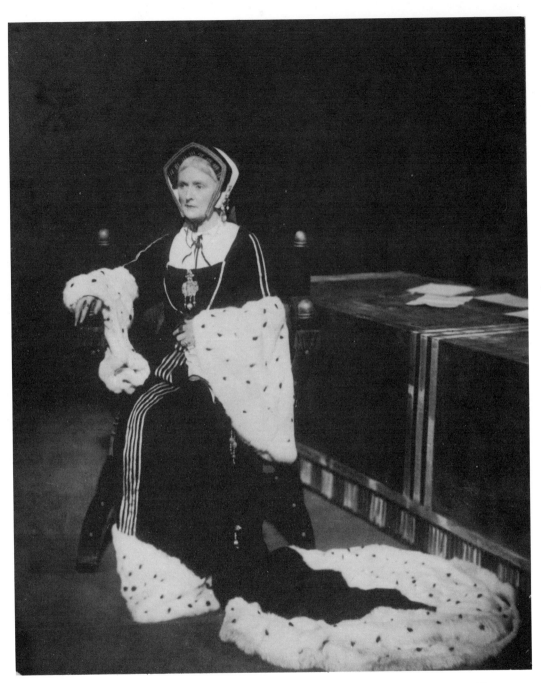

in 1928. 'This year I dressed a Mystery Play in Canterbury
Cathedral, and although all the work was done by ama-
teurs the result was proclaimed superb by all who saw it.
I made some twelve crowns including an elaborate Van-
Eyck-looking one in rock crystal, pearls and rubies, and
over twenty brooches or cope clasps, jewelled shoes, etc.,
etc., and this doll of the Holy Child. I secured first-rate
properties shields and banners from the local art school,

Above: Sybil Thorndike as
Katharine of Aragon in *Henry
VIII.*

Right: Costume design for Cecil
Lewis's *Montezuma c*1925.

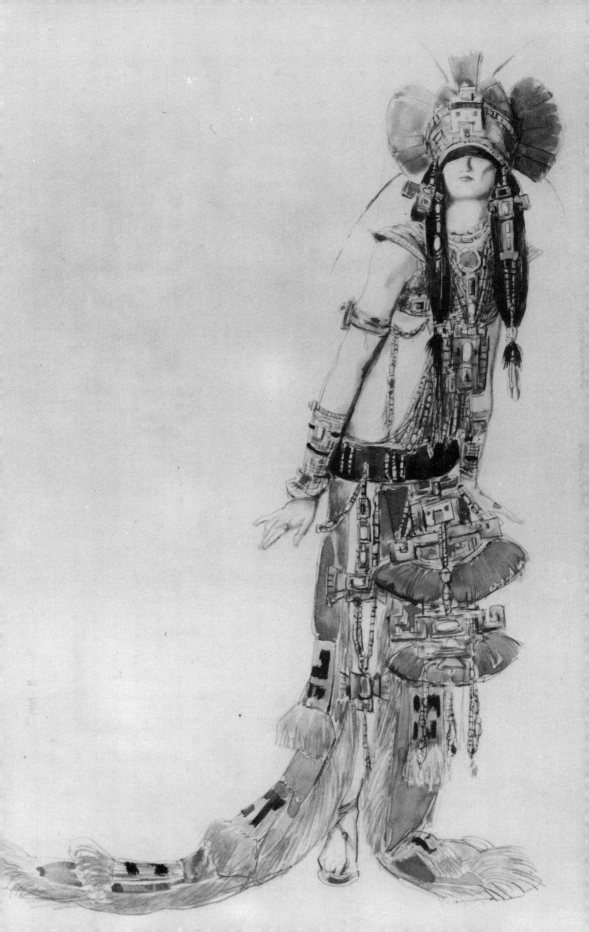

and had the huge choir steps of Canterbury and the screen for a setting. I dressed Christ entirely in white, and red and white jewels, the archangels in gold, the girl-angels and Holy Virgin in Gentian blue, the warriors in steel and blood; the diplomat king wore one of the most finished and beautiful dresses I have seen, white ribbed silk decorated with heraldic bands of ermine (I made the ermine tails myself), with white jewelled gloves and shoes lined throughout with crimson, his Giles de Retz head-dress of scarlet velvet with delicate jewels.'

As a costume designer Ricketts was prolific. Cecil Lewis remembered seeing him create forty drawings for a production in one day. 'They were dashed off rapidly on foolscap and thrown on the floor. Subsequently, with his foot, he would move them about, grouping together characters who would appear on the stage together, to judge if their colour and accent would be effective, and altering if the need arose.' He enjoyed working on designs and properties. Painting the figure of Christ for John Masefield's *Philip the King* was, he said, the sort of trivial job he liked and enjoyed. His facility gained him several surprising offers by which he was flattered, but which he was certainly not prepared to accept. They included staging productions at the Gaiety Theatre, and acting as adviser to Lucille, a leading couturier.

His stage settings evolved from early ideas formed in discussion with Oscar Wilde, to historical panoramas, impressive settings for Shakespeare and even opera. Lillah McCarthy, an enthusiastic admirer of his settings, judged

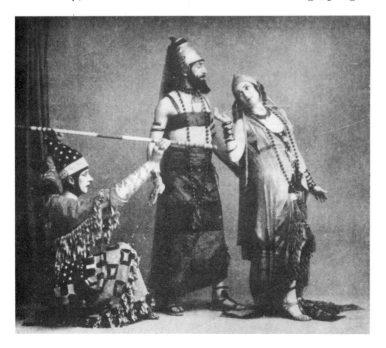

Judith by Arnold Bennett, staged at the Kingsway Theatre in 1919. Lillah McCarthy as Judith standing right.

178

Norman McKinnell as Lear in
King Lear, designed by Ricketts
for the Haymarket Theatre,
1909.

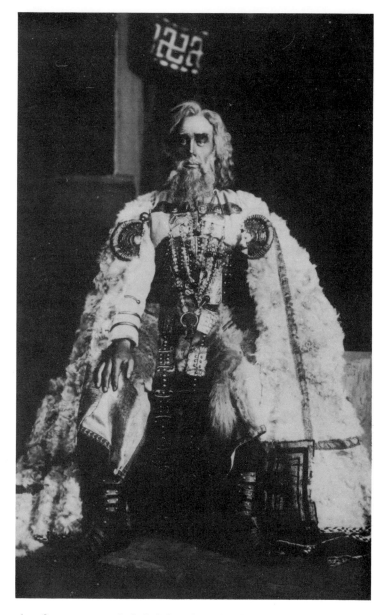

the first scene of *Judith* by Arnold Bennett (produced in
1919) 'Surely one of the more beautiful ever designed – it
showed the great bronze gates and towers of the besieged
city, and when you looked upon it hunger could be seen
walking the streets.' Ricketts, however, did not enjoy working on a narrow stage, nineteen feet deep, into which he
had to fit 'a town, a town gate and Judith's house in the
first act, plus a crowd of thirty people and a dance of six
clumsy girls.' He liked the opportunity of working on a
grand scale, or creating effects of grandeur. For *King Lear*
in 1909, he designed the interiors in a massive, mystical
architecture inspired by Stonehenge. 'These are certainly

179

the most impressive and appropriate settings that anyone has devised for this supreme play.' He was happy at Covent Garden: '*Philip the King* remains one of my favourite sets. The Covent Garden stage allowed scale and space, both rare in London theatres. I remember with pleasure the huge semi-circle of curtains, the monumental doors studded with coffin nails, the huge crucified Christ I painted in the manner of El Greco.' John Masefield was appreciative of the setting his play had been given, and wrote to Ricketts 'I thought your room, with the Greco and the hangings, the most splendid scene I have ever seen.'

When it came to the costumes themselves, Ricketts did not forget the actor or actresses who was to wear the clothes. He might think of a dress as a design, perhaps something as strange, exotic or bizarre as the costume worn by Lillah McCarthy as Judith in 1919: 'Lillah's bare torso, covered with bands and straps of jewels, emerging from the fishtail skirt, the jewelled leg also bare, would have enchanted Gustave Moreau.' (This dress was banned by the Lord Chamberlain in his capacity as theatrical censor.) He clearly enjoyed the artistic challenge of, say, Japanese or Aztec costume, but always remained sensitive to such practical considerations as effects of movement on stage. He provided Lillah McCarthy with detailed advice when designing her dress for a charity performance of *The Admirable Crichton* (1916) in aid of King George's Pension Fund:

'I want you to be very free of movement with your legs (the dress is designed for that). Do not hesitate to toss your hair about and sleek it with your hand from time to time, it is a charming action. When you put on your necklace and wreath you should play with your hair; then become absorbed and give a little sigh as you turn to the punka. You must, in fact, suggest an island Rosalind throughout the act in all your movements, with a moment when you are more feminine than Rosalind. Be very free with the movements of your head; the other ladies will not. The dress is intended to suggest a rough active life, the flowers are there because you are in love.

'Don't think me pompous and out of my business when I beg you to remember this even in your hunting speeches; in these be wreathed with smiles; you must glitter and fascinate.

'There is danger in the "slavey" speech (where you rub your hands). I should advise you to look down and upwards, as if hardly conscious of the words.

'I am saying this, as the size of the stage and the audience may have led you, and your advisers, into too much technique and the making of points. The other lovely ladies

Right: Lillah McCarthy portrayed by Sir John Lavery, in an admirably fluent study, as Lady Mary in *The Admirable Crichton* by J.M. Barrie.

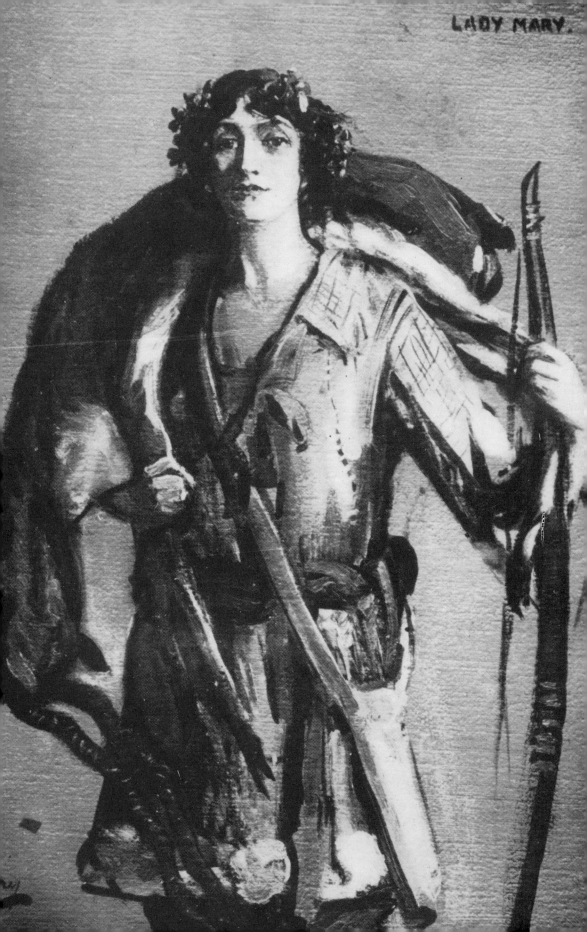

LADY MARY.

have nothing to do or say, save trust to their popular personalities. You are in love, radiant with health and vitality, but softened by being in love, when, in the former acts, you have been dormant and indifferent or thrown upon yourself.

'Forgive this lecture it grows out of the dress. You were thinking of him when you picked the berries and flowers in your rough dress.'

Lillah McCarthy replied to her 'most adored friend' that 'The results were satisfactory and I am repaid, though I cursed the idiots in charge of the stage for lowering the lights in Act III and extinguishing the beauties of your lovely dress, so that I was the chief person to enjoy all its detail. They sprung that darkness on me, I had no idea they were going to play such a dirty trick. Your letter came in time to take me entirely out of my anxious state, and melt me into a passionate mood . . .' and went on with a vow to 'raise money by fair means or foul' to produce a play, should Ricketts suggest one for her.

Lillah McCarthy's autobiography is one of many sources of comment on the rapport between Ricketts and Shannon. She cites an occasion when Shannon painted her portrait, to which Ricketts calmly added a butterfly in her head-dress. Of Ricketts she writes, 'Once I had been impatient with my dressmaker for the way she worked on his design. "Don't scold or punish people," he wrote. And in that phrase he revealed the key to his human relationships. Unerring historical knowledge gave his criticism force, but the force was never cruel.' One of the achievements of her own career was to bring Shaw's heroines to life. Shaw's requirements for an actress were not those of the commercial theatre of his day; what pleased him in Lillah McCarthy was that she had been ' . . . saturated with declamatory poetry and rhetoric from her cradle . . . She was beautiful, plastic, statuesque, most handsomely made, and seemed to have come straight from the Italian or eighteenth century stage without a trace of the stuffiness of the London cup-and-saucer theatre.'

Like his friendship with Shaw, the close relationship Ricketts formed with Lillah McCarthy's husband, Granville Barker, was essential to his theatrical career. Barker was not only an actor and a playwright of note, he was an outstanding producer. Ricketts's first theatrical designs for him were created for the production of *A Miracle* by the Literary Theatre Society in 1907. They got on well, and Ricketts designed dresses for Lillah McCarthy in Shaw's *Arms and the Man*, co-produced by Barker in the same year. Five years later, Ricketts designed costumes for Maeterlinck's *Death of Tintagiles*. In 1914 he completed

Right: Shannon's portrait of Lillah McCarthy as the Dumb Wife in Anatole France's *The Man Who Married a Dumb Wife*, complete with Ricketts' butterfly on her headdress.

182

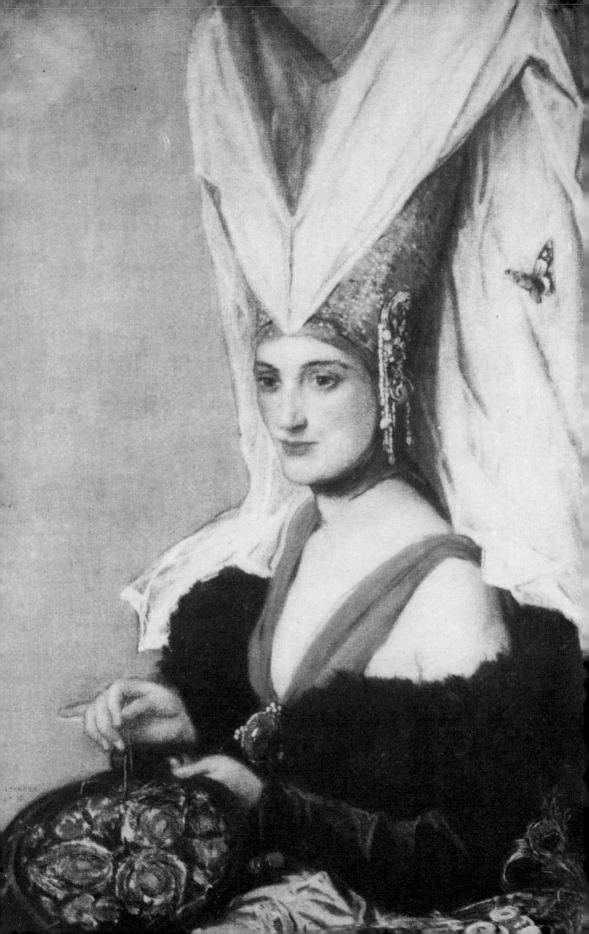

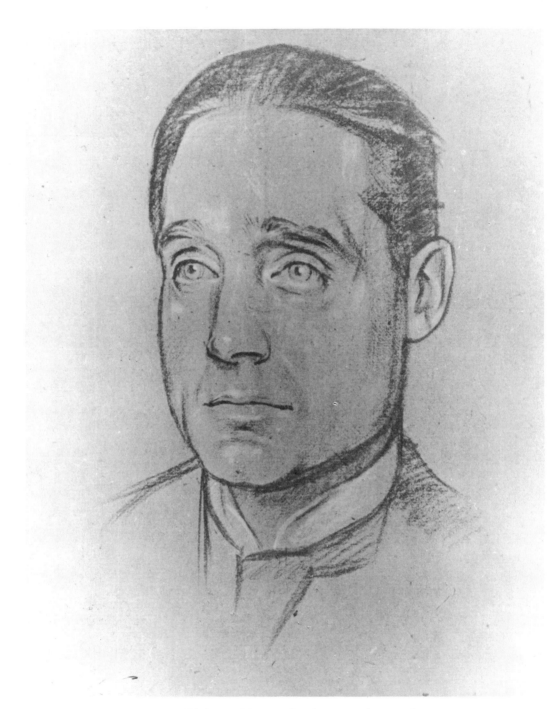

designs for *Philip the King*. Ricketts felt that Barker was the best producer that the English theatre had seen since Irving, and shared the widespread dismay in London at Barker's decision to leave the theatre in 1923 to become the Director of the British Institute in Paris. Their last collaboration was Maurice Maeterlinck's *The Betrothal*, staged at the Gaiety Theatre in 1921.

Above: Harley Granville Barker by William Rothenstein.

Opposite, above: two Ricketts' costumes for Maeterlinck's *Death of Tintagiles.* Odette Goimbault (left). Lillah McCarthy (right).

184

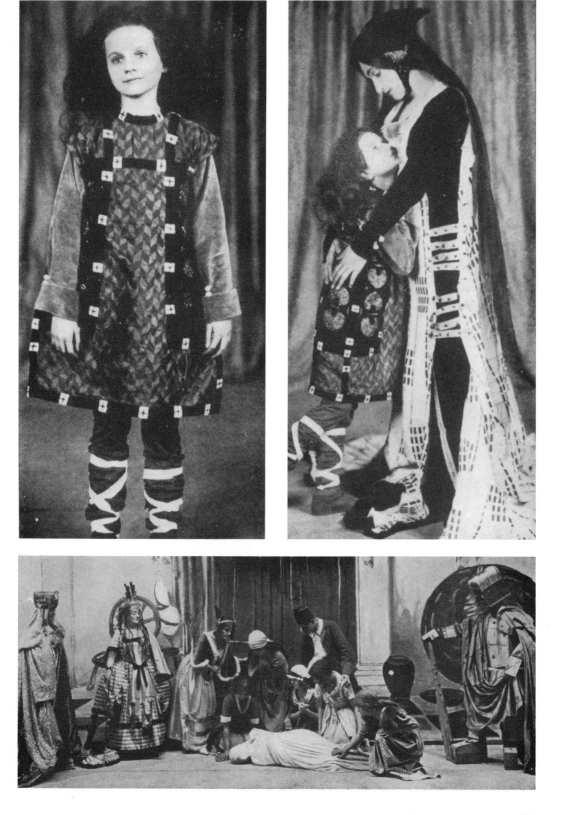

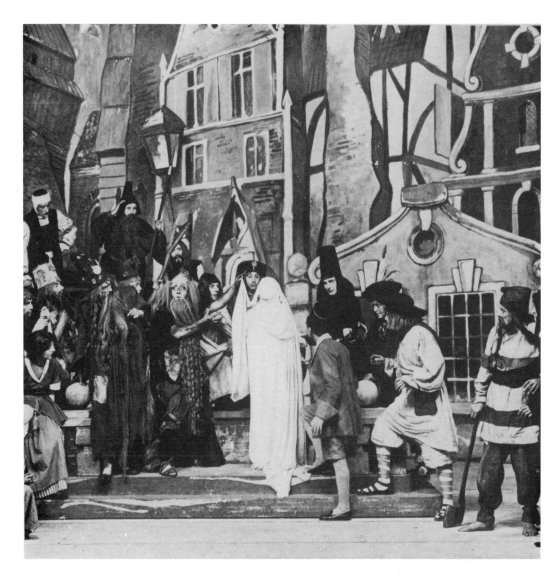

Previous page, below, & this page, above: Ricketts designed the sets and costumes for this production of Maeterlinck's *The Betrothal,* 1921.

Ricketts kept good company in the theatre, designing costumes for Mrs Patrick Campbell, Penelope Wheeler and Sybil Thorndike, as well as Lillah McCarthy. He managed to retain his connection with the poetic drama that had first drawn him to theatrical work. He designed several productions for the Irish Players, among them W. B. Yeats's *The King's Threshold* in 1914. Yeats formed a high opinion of Ricketts, of whom he wrote after his death 'One of the lights that lit my dark house has gone.' Ricketts followed his work on *The King's Threshold* with designs for *On Baile's Strand* produced at the Little Theatre.

Although he would certainly have made a fine designer for opera on a grand scale, Ricketts turned down tentative offers from Bayreuth. He was never offered the opportunity to design for Mozart's *Magic Flute*, which he mentions in

186

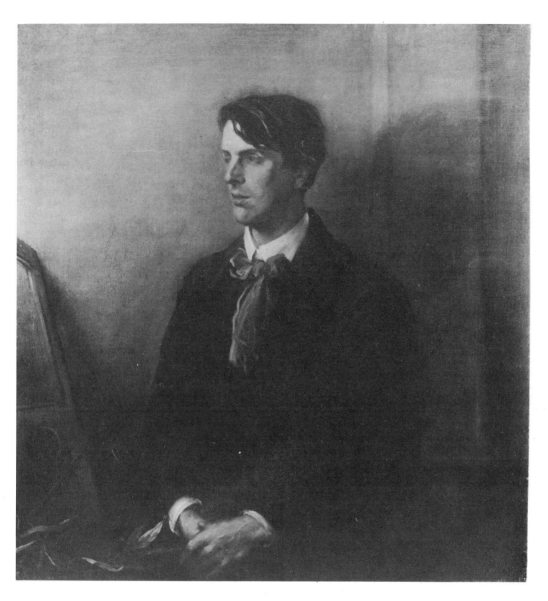

Above: William Butler Yeats
portrayed by Shannon.

his diary as a production he would have liked to work on,
and the small-scale operatic performances by the Russian
tenor Vladimir Rosing gave him little scope. However, he
accepted commissions from the D'Oyly Carte Company to
design for *The Mikado* and *The Gondoliers*. His expert knowledge was invaluable for the Japanese costumes:

'In the *Mikado* everything turned out perfectly in execution,
the dresses being the most successful I have so far done.
With the exception of Katisha – who hated her dress – all
the women looked exquisite. Binyon was overwhelmed.
The men, I regret to say, excepting Koko and Pooh Bah,
were paralysed by their clothes and looked dressed up. The
public on the first night, and the public since, have been

187

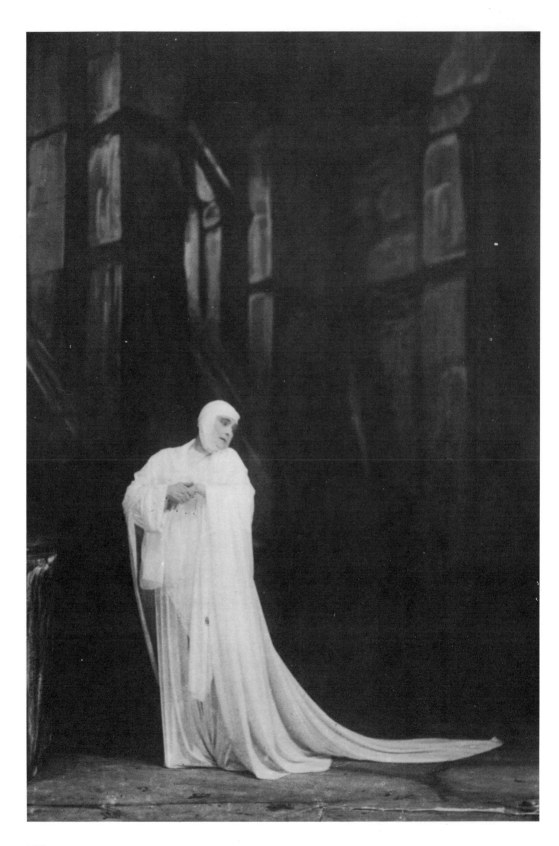

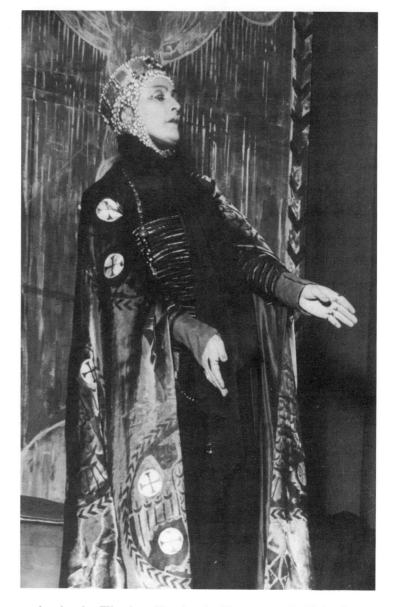

Left & right: Two stunning costumes designed by Ricketts for Sybil Thorndike as Lady Macbeth in *Macbeth* directed by Lewis Casson at the Prince's Theatre, 1926.

enthusiastic. The hostility in the Press was, I think, due to some dozen interviews I gave to as many pressmen at Townshend House in the dining-room before D'Oyly Carte. I think they thought me a gentle lunatic, but praised the drawings; hence sniffs and dispraise among the musical critics.' Gordon Bottomley emphasised the popular praise – he claimed that Ricketts's designs were 'sufficient reason for a deaf man to attend a performance of the operetta.'

The characteristic that would have made Ricketts particularly suited to designing for opera was his great love for music. True, he did design for Isodore de Lara's *Nail*, conducted by Sir Thomas Beecham and produced in 1919,

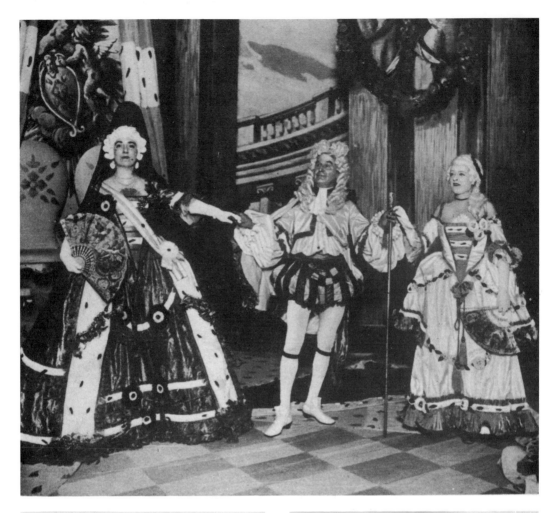

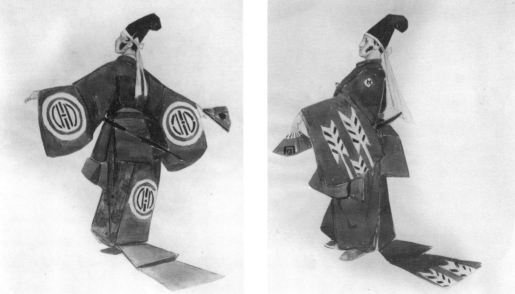

190

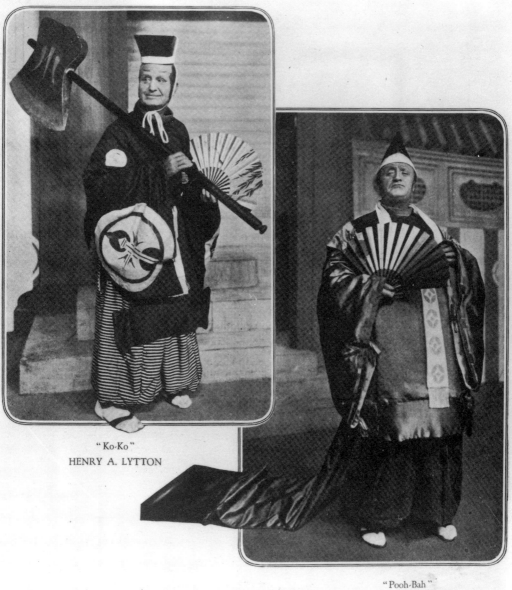

"Ko-Ko"
HENRY A. LYTTON

"Pooh-Bah"
LEO SHEFFIELD

Left, above: Ricketts redressed this D'Oyly Carte production of *The Gondoliers. Left, below, and this page:* Costumes designed for *The Mikado* staged in 1926.

but the great classical repertoire would have suited him magnificently. Analogies in the arts occured naturally to him, and his insight into the character of some of the great composers would have been valuable:

'Beethoven, with his sorrows, prayers, gaiety, and consolations, urges you to endure the possibilities of passion and regret. Was Bach, the sedentary and solitary Bach, even more sensitive? Sensitive is not the word, possibly. "Sentient" is better. In a formula of pure pattern and ornament one becomes aware of a thousand exquisite

191

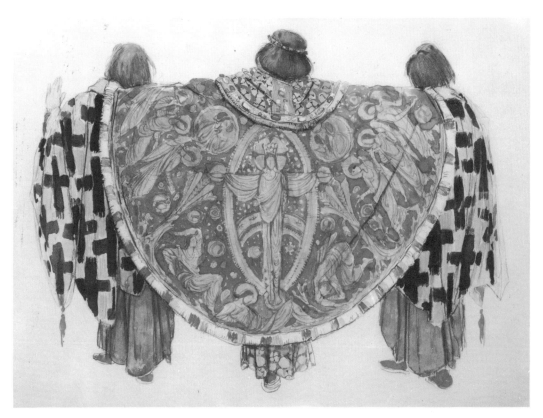

things crumbling away like the glittering mist from a fountain. The Adagio of the D major concerto left me almost
as shattered as if I had been listening to the nerve-racking
sounds of Wagner, in which physical strain counts for so
much. Baudelaire compares Chopin's music to the flight of
a glistening bird over an abyss. This summarises the effect
of a great deal of the finest music – the first movement, for
instance, of Beethoven's great concerto for the violin.' In
the interpretation, as opposed to the writing, of music,
Chaliapin impressed him as; 'The finest dramatic actor of
my lifetime . . . to power, tone, presence, to all the instinctive qualities, he adds a profound and studied naturalness,
a great variety, and the most subtle qualities of imaginative
insight and a source of beauty which must spring from a
fine and generous nature . . . I know no quality belonging
to an actor's art, from brutality to tenderness, which Chaliapin does not possess; he seems boundless in resource . . .'
The expression of such enthusiasm makes it easier to understand Ricketts's dismissal of Shaw's musical criticism.
'Shaw's wicked musical *boutades* are not wholly untrue, he
seems rather to understand music without really liking it
– probably, like God, he rather dislikes everything.'

Ricketts rather dreaded Shaw's influence on one of his
friends, the young writer Cecil Lewis, whom he had met

at the flat of Vladimir Rosing, from whom Lewis was taking music lessons. Ricketts encouraged his attempt to earn a living as a writer in the 1920s, completing designs that were among the most splendid in his career for Lewis's play about Montezuma, in the hope of increasing the chances of its being performed. Lewis went on to write about his experience as a pilot in World War I in *Sagittarius Rising* (1936), and edited *Self-portrait*, the selection from Rickett's letters and diaries published in 1939.

A measure of the power achieved by Ricketts in his stage settings and costume is recaptured in his original drawings for the theatre, of which more than three hundred have fortunately found their way into public collections. The designs were bought after his death and distributed by the National Art Collections Fund, with which he had been involved since its foundation. They give at least an idea of the splendour and variety of his theatrical creations. The costume drawings in particular express a fluency that is much in contrast with his hesitations as a painter. The costumes are elegant notations, verging on a fashionable chic, in which the pose sets off the costume but rarely characterises the role. They possess what many readers like in illustrations to a novel, sufficient definition to stimulate imagination but not enough to fix an image or to challenge a reader's own conception. Ricketts's drawings for settings are more definite, stressing the quality of mood he wished to convey: for *Saint Joan*, he designed an elaborate theatre curtain with the detail of a medieval tapestry to create an atmosphere even before the start of the play.

In publishing his essay on the art of stage decoration in 1913, Ricketts was not only speaking from experience but also, in part, looking to the future. His involvement with poetic drama, the main subject of his career in theatrical design, had awakened him to what he felt were unrealised possibilities:

'Can all these moods of the poetic and lyric stage fall under the control of a few principles and rules? They can only in so far as that their treatment remains "non-realistic", like the text itself, be the method used an insistence upon mass, line, tone, colour, detail or even the use of light, which art never marshalled, focussed or brought into interrelation by our English managers. We hear the word "simplicity" used too often as a guiding principle; I am not sure I have not used it too often myself. A beautiful setting should "seem" simple when this is the character demanded by the play, not otherwise. Underlying the simplicity or complexity demanded by the progress or development of the piece, the artist must husband his resources, reveal or conceal detail, much as a composer marshals and controls an orchestra, or a painter the composing elements of a picture.'

193

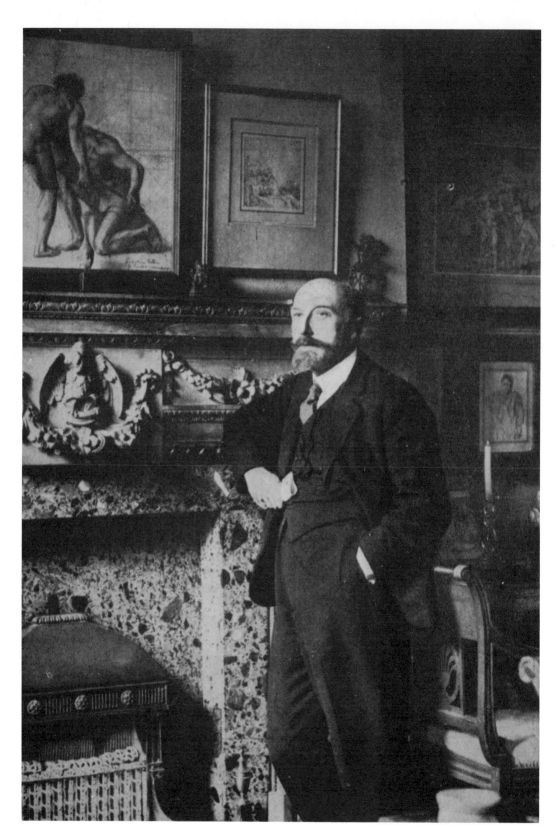

With such evident qualities as a designer, Ricketts de-
served greater fulfilment of his potential than opportunity
allowed. As Ifan Kyrle Fletcher has pointed out, the position of an artistic director in the English theatre was made
more difficult by the commercial organisation of theatrical
production. Ricketts could not equal the limitless energy
that enabled Diaghilev to make his own opportunities; he
could not find the individual backing or resources that were
available to Edward Gordon Craig in the German theatre.
Fletcher put the point clearly: 'The National Theatre, of
which it seemed that Barker was the natural founder and
director, would have had in Ricketts an artistic director of
masterly power. In such a setting his mature imagination,
his critical tact and his generous spirit would have found
their rightful place. The disaster which robbed the English
theatre of Barker was a disaster also for Ricketts. There
was no place for him, and he made the best of it, accepting
the means that lay to hand.'

Ricketts's character was not matched, he felt with his
times. In a conversational game with his friends, he as-
signed to each person a place and a period. Holmes's solid
intelligence made him a seventeenth-century Dutchman,
Shannon was a Renaissance Venetian, while Ricketts
would have been at home in the France of Henry III. That
last court of the Valois survived in fifteen years of constant
stress in French society, distinguished by elaborate court
ballets, rigorous religious exercises and recondite poetry.
The choice of period conveys Ricketts's sense of the fragility
of art, for was not beauty only 'a moment of harmony
between opposites, hardly more enduring than music'? It
suggests, too, that although art could be out of key with its
time, this lack of sympathy would be treated by the artist
as a matter of indifference. A feeling of neglect was part of
Ricketts's character, but he did not fall into self-pity. He
had a vivid sense of the value of life 'with its enthralling
conflicts of light, shadow and change', which inspired
friends and colleagues. He wished that he had been a
greater artist. Perhaps he would have become reconciled
to a lesser role as an impresario, or a gallery director? In
the end, we can understand Ricketts's hints of regret at not
fulfilling himself, while admiring the courage and quality
of his life.

Bibliography

Books are cited for the first chapter in which a quotation appears.

Chapter 1.

Charles Ricketts, RA, Sixty five Designs, introduction by T. Sturge Moore, 1933. (This personal memoir is indispensable.)

W. B. Yeats & T. Sturge Moore, their correspondence 1901–1937, edited by Ursula Bridge, 1953.

Charles Ricketts, *Self Portrait*, taken from his letters and journals, collected and compiled by T. Sturge Moore and edited by Cecil Lewis, 1939. (The major published source for information about Charles Ricketts, from which many quotations in this book are drawn.)

Stephen Calloway, *Charles Ricketts*, with a Foreword by Lord Clark, 1979. (This recent survey of Ricketts' art and designs has a useful bibliography.)

C. J. Holmes, *Self and Partners (Mostly Self)*, 1936.

William Rothenstein, *Men and Memories*, 1912–1922, 1931–1932 (2 volumes).

Charles Ricketts, Michael Field, edited by Paul Delaney, Edinburgh 1976.

Mary Sturgeon, *Michael Field*, 1922.

Chapter 2.

Charles Ricketts, *Recollections of Oscar Wilde*, 1932

Charles Ricketts, *Pages on Art*, 1913.

Gleeson White, *Moreau*, in *The Pageant*, 1897.

Charles Ricketts, *A Bibliography of the books issued by Hacon & Ricketts*, 1904. (The last book from the Vale Press was issued in 1903, so that this Bibliography of the Press was issued privately.)

Charles Ricketts, *A Note on Original Wood-Engraving*, in *The Pageant*, 1897.

Chapter 3.

Walter Sickert, *A Free House*, edited by Osbert Sitwell, 1947.

John Fothergill, *My Three Inns*, 1949.

Chapter 4.

T. Sturge Moore, *Armour for Aphrodite*, 1929.

C. J. Holmes, *Notes on the Science of Picture Making*, 1909.

Charles Ricketts, *Titian*, 1910.

T. Sturge Moore, *Correggio*, 1906

Sidney Colvin, *Memories and Notes*, 1921.

Chapter 5.

Charles Ricketts, *The Prado and its Masterpieces*, 1903.

Chapter 7.

Friend of Friends, edited by Margery Ross, 1952 (on Robert Ross).

Friends of a Lifetime: more letters to Sidney Carlyle Cockerell, edited by Viola Meynell, 1940.

Chapter 8.

C. J. Holmes, *Hokusai*, 1899.

Chapter 9.

Ifan Kyrle Fletcher, *Charles Ricketts and the Theatre*, in *Theatre Notebook* XXII, no 1, Autumn 1967.

Lillah McCarthy, *Myself and My Friends*, 1933.

Jean Paul Raymond (Charles Ricketts), *Beyond the Threshold*, 1929.

SELECTED BOOKS AND CATALOGUES

S. L. Behrman, *Duveen*, 1952.

Laurence Binyon, *Catalogue of the Japanese and Chinese Woodcuts in the British Museum*, 1916.

Stephen Calloway and Paul Delaney, *Charles Ricketts and Charles Shannon: an aesthetic partnership* (exhibition catalogue), Twickenham, 1979.

Joseph Darracott, *All for Art: the Ricketts and Shannon Collection* (at the Fitzwilliam Museum, Cambridge, an exhibition catalogue edited by Joseph Darracott), Cambridge 1979.

Paul Delaney, *The Lithographs of Charles Shannon* (exhibition catalogue with an introduction by Fenella Crichton), Taranman Gallery, London 1978.

Michael Field, *Works and Days*, edited by T. Sturge Moore, 1933.

Colin Franklin, *The Private Presses*, 1969.

Roger Fry, Letters, edited by Denys Sutton, 2 vols, 1972.

C. J. Holmes, *Pictures and Picture Collecting*, 1910.

Holbrook Jackson, *The Eighteen Nineties*, 1922.

S. Legge, *Affectionate Cousins*, 1980. (An admirably documented account of Thomas Sturge Moore and his wife.)

Cecil Lewis, *Never Look Back*, 1974.

T. Sturge Moore, *A brief account of the origins of the Eragny Press*, 1933.

William Morris, *A Note by William Morris on his aims in founding the Kelmscott Press* (with a description of the Press by S. C. Cockerell), 1898.

Gerald Reitlinger, *The Economics of Taste*, Vol 2, 1963.

Charles Ricketts et Lucien Pissarro, *De la Typographie et de l'harmonie de la page imprimée. William Morris et son influence sur les arts et metiers*, 1898

Charles Ricketts, *A Defence of the Revival of Printing*, 1899.

E. Samuelson, *Berenson, the Beginnings of a Connoisseur*, 1979 (with a bibliography).

John Russell Taylor, *The Art Nouveau Book in Britain*, 1966. (This book contains a perceptive and enthusiastic account of Ricketts' work as a book designer.)

Frank Whitford, *Japanese Prints and Western Painters*, 1977.

UNPUBLISHED SOURCES

The main source of unpublished material for this study is the collection of the papers of Charles Ricketts and Charles Shannon at the British Library, where they have been carefully ordered by Miss Janet Backhouse Key words for quotations in different chapters are given with the manuscript number against them. For quotations from the archive of the National Gallery of Canada, the correspondents and a date or suggested date is given.

Chapter 1.
Un ami se lasse (58092); Cinders. Ashes. Dust. (58099); He talked well (58102); the poem (58087).

Chapter 3.
I thought most of the pictures (58102).

Chapter 4.
I do not look forward (58089); the famous alterpiece (58085).

Chapter 6.
He was a very great person (Brown-King, Oct 28, 1931); in Venetian pictures (Ricketts-King, 1930); our Tintoretto (Ricketts-Brown, 1930); I believe we should get (Brown-Walker, May 28, 1923); a very serious (Ricketts-Brown, 1924); The Stubbs *Death of a Doe* (Ricketts-Brown, 1924); in the sale rooms (Ricketts-Brown, August 1923); in a sense purchases (Ricketts-Brown, August 1923); huge prices obtained (Ricketts-Brown, August 1926); I like the Reynolds (Ricketts-Brown, December 1925); the 'Vermeer' (Ricketts-Brown, Jan 18 1924); his collection is very varied (Ricketts, Sept 1928); I suppose you could not get (Ricketts-Brown, July 1927); Colin has discovered (Ricketts-Brown, Sept 1926); I expect Colin Agnew (Brown-Ricketts, Sept 10, 1926); will be good people being tired (Ricketts-Brown, Nov 1928); I will write to Mr Southam (Ricketts-Brown, Feb 27, 1931); H. S. Southam (Brown-Ricketts, Nov 12, 1929); within the last few weeks (Ricketts-Brown, Sept 25, 1925); Perroneau is greatly to the fore (Ricketts-Brown, Oct 1925); from the big museum point of view (Ricketts-Brown, Dec 1925); the tragedy is the Perroneau (58085); I would not advise (Ricketts-Brown, 1925); should an extra grant be necessary (Ricketts-Brown, March 1930); I hear Duveen (Brown-Ricketts, Nov 21, 1928); Frank Wood has had no difficulty (Brown-Ricketts, April 4, 1928); I feel I have left the pack (Ricketts); You are the man.

Chapter 7.
feeble in workmanship; Met Mrs Gardner.

Index